BETTAS

A COMPLETE INTRODUCTION

Walt Maurus

T.F.H. Publications, Inc.
One TFH Plaza
Third and Union Avenues
Neptune City, NJ 07753

This book has been published with the intent to provide accurate
and authoritative information in regard to the subject matter
within. While every precaution has been taken in preparation of
this book, the publisher and author assume no responsibility for
errors or omissions. Neither is any liability assumed for damages
resulting from the use of the information herein.

ISBN 0-86622-288-X

www.tfh.com

TABLE OF CONTENTS

BETTAS—A COMPLETE INTRODUCTION

INTRODUCTION

Love with an abiding interest often evades a truly communicative description. At best, an attempt at description might still leave the reader with only a superficial understanding and, perhaps, no real meaning. However, a writer must at least try to accomplish just that if he wishes to share with others the experience of love and to provide motivation for others to enjoy it also. It is hoped that what is offered here will at least in some small part begin to accomplish this.

One of the protests most often heard in our hobby is that the commonly available references offer little that coincides with the fish-keeping experiences of reader-hobbyists. In most cases, those who protest have experienced exceptions to the cited "rules," and they come to assume, therefore, that the generalizations offered are wrong. Because many changes and additions in the information we have come along constantly, the "rules" cited in this offering may soon

The fascinating breeding habits and brilliant colors of the common betta or Siamese fighting fish, *Betta splendens*, have combined to make it one of the most beloved and abundant tropical fish.

After almost a century of selective breeding by dedicated hobbyists and commercial producers, bettas now come in literally dozens of colors and many different fin shapes.

be obsolete. Be that as it may, this book is offered for what it may be worth to the reader, and it is hoped that some day the reader will gather knowledge and then be willing to share what was learned.

This writer has worked with bettas for a number of years and during this time has been asked many questions about them. These questions have usually dealt with very basic aspects of the keeping and breeding of bettas, and the same questions continue to be asked. This book will reflect the content of answers given to those questions, based on personal experiences with the fish and communications received from many others who also enjoy bettas. They tell of their enjoyment of the betta for its beauty and its extremely interesting breeding pattern, and they tell also of their great pride in raising good fry and the variety to be found in the colors possible with this fish. Therefore, much credit must go to all hobbyists who respond to the betta in all its glory.

BETTAS—A COMPLETE INTRODUCTION

WHAT IS A BETTA?

The Siamese fighting fish, *Betta splendens*, as we know it today is so far removed in appearance from its original wild ancestor (described by Theodor E. Cantor in 1849) that to all but experienced aquarists it does not appear to be the same species. Although many years of careful selective breeding have vastly modified the drab, uninteresting wild *Betta* into a spectacular fish with long flowing fins and vivid colors, certain behavioral characteristics and anatomical features of today's *Betta splendens* allow it to be unquestionably classified as a member of the suborder Anabantoidei.

All anabantoids have a labyrinth or accessory breathing organ. All but a few of these fishes are found residing in hot, steamy, oxygen-deficient swamps in tropical Asia and Africa.

The many groups of labyrinth fishes, most of them known as gouramis, often are arranged in families and subfamilies as follows:

Suborder: Anabantoidei

Family: Anabantidae
    Genera: *Anabas, Ctenopoma, Sandelia*
Family: Osphronemidae
    Genus: *Osphronemus*
Family: Helostomatidae
    Genus: *Helostoma*
Family: Belontiidae
    Subfamily: Belontiinae
      Genus: *Belontia*
    Subfamily: Macropodinae
      Genera: *Betta, Ctenops, Macropodus, Malpulutta, Parosphromenus, Trichopsis*
    Subfamily: Trichogasterinae
      Genera: *Colisa, Parasphaerichthys, Sphaerichthys, Trichogaster.*

Belontia signata, though not colorful and highly aggressive, is one of the most familiar anabantoids and a close relative of the bettas.

Hobbyists maintain over a dozen wild betta species, some attractive, some not exactly exciting to the casual hobbyist. This is *Betta bellica*, an interesting fish with few bright colors.

In addition to *Betta splendens*, the genus *Betta* contains somewhere over two dozen other species, the exact number depending on the opinion of individual ichthyologists, who differ in which species they regard as valid. *Betta splendens* and the very closely allied (some ichthyologists consider them identical, in fact) *B. smaragdina* and *B. imbellis* are bubblenest builders, but all or almost all of the other *Betta* species are mouthbrooders. (Bubblenest builders place their eggs in a nest of air bubbles on the surface; mouthbrooders hold the eggs in their mouth until they hatch.) Among the other *Betta* species, those occasionally seen by hobbyists include: *B. bellica*, *B. brederi*, *B. anabatoides*, *B. picta*, *B. unimaculata*, *B. tessyae*, *B. edithae*, *B. coccina*, *B. macrostoma*, *B. foerschi*, *B. pugnax*, *B. akarensis*, *B. taeniata*, and *B. fasciata*.

BETTAS—A COMPLETE INTRODUCTION

Keeping Bettas

WATER SPACE AND CONTAINERS

The great majority of people who purchase bettas do so in order to add beauty and grace to their community tanks or to their divided betta tanks. Others, however, keep single male bettas in appropriate containers; many times these fish become, as close as any fish can become, pets. Bettas, being labyrinth fish, are ideal for keeping in small containers. Minimum maintenance will keep bettas in good health. They can be kept successfully in glass or plastic containers that might be assumed to be too small or confining for other tropicals and even other anabantoids. Canning jars, goldfish bowls, tumblers and snifters, candy jars and so on can serve excellently. Bettas require only that they be fed proper foods regularly and sufficiently and that their water be kept clean. Keeping them well fed and clean, coupled with the fact that they are labyrinth fish, makes bettas more successfully kept than goldfish in similarly sized quarters. As you know, goldfish often succumb to oxygen deficiency in small quarters, but since bettas can obtain their needs by coming to the surface for air, they are perfectly content in water space that would very quickly put a goldfish in oxygen distress. It can readily be assumed that bettas could very well be selected for color that might harmonize with a home or room color scheme. They might be of a color that would emphasize a dominant color in a room or contrast with it in order to accent it.

A betta can exist in a very small water space, but not for long without a water change. The smaller the water space the more often the need for a water change. A quart of water, for instance, needs changing under normal conditions at least once a week, and this seems to be about the minimum of water to be recommended. Bettas can be kept in food or canning jars, but a little imagination might suggest more interesting containers. Very exotic containers might be found, and somebody handy with tools might design and build containers of glass and plastic.

Bettas can tolerate many differences in water. A change of water need only be the same temperature, usually, as the old water, and the new water need only be aged one day to be usable. In many parts of the country, the water is safe right from the tap without aging or with the use of chlorine neutralizers as long as temperature is considered. If well water or extremes of pH or hardness are found, steps must be taken. Bettas, being bettas, can tolerate much—but they can be thrown into shock and killed if a water change is too extreme.

Water need not be filtered when bettas are kept singly in small containers, but filtering does lengthen

Yes, you really can keep a single male betta in a quart jar or bowl—but the water must be changed often and the room must be kept warm. A real aquarium is better than any betta bowl.

periods between needed water changes. Small filters are available for small containers. A lessening of activity can indicate that the fish needs a water change. An increase of activity is noted when water is changed. Air stones are not needed for bettas. Gravel, plants, and other decorative materials can be used, but they are not necessary.

If a betta seems to be listless even if the above conditions are given, adding salt to the water at the rate of a tablespoon for each gallon of water can help. The salt should be non-iodized. Give a water change two or three days later and repeat the salt treatment if necessary. Be watchful for signs of disease.

FOODS

Bettas are not too fussy about daily fare as long as it is regular and in adequate amounts. Frozen or live adult brine shrimp, newly hatched live brine shrimp, tubifex or white worms, microworms, mosquito larvae, daphnia, bits of raw beef or liver and even hamburger (not recommended) might be taken. Find out what the fish you buy have been accustomed to; if it is necessary to change the fish's diet, do so gradually. A varied diet is better than a reliance on one food. Dried foods should be used only as a supplement to the above. Freeze-dried foods are good, but the fish should be given time to become accustomed to them.

One feeding a day does not seem to be adequate no matter what type of food is fed. Two, three, and even more feedings a day have been reported by breeders using different foods at each feeding. One heavy feeding is not usually consumed completely, resulting in foul water and the danger of weakening the fish. So we must ask what kinds of foods should be fed, how many times a day and in what amounts. Some experimentation will help to decide very quickly what foods produce good fish and how often the fish will eat

You can maintain a betta by giving it a variety of prepared foods, but supplementing this monotonous diet with live foods is always best.

　　　　　　　　　　BETTAS—A COMPLETE INTRODUCTION

Almost all fish shops carry living tubifex worms, which make a great addition to the diet of any betta. Be sure the worms are clean and alive before feeding. Clean the aquarium after feeding tubifex to keep them from moving into the gravel.

all the food offered. However, the fish should not be "killed with kindness." There is scientific evidence that bettas should live much longer than the commonly held belief that they live about two years. I have had some bettas for more than three years. While bettas are growing, they must be fed in amounts to ensure growth and good health.

Almost all breeders of bettas use prepared foods, usually of a meat and cereal combination. Some are cooked and some are not. Such meats as chicken liver, beef heart and liver, horsemeat, dog and cat foods, and fishmeal have been reported. Various methods have been devised for feeding these foods. Frozen foods are chopped, scraped or melted and fed with an eyedropper, and so on.

TEMPERATURE

Bettas are considered tropical fish, but they can be kept satisfactorily at 70 degrees F. but also up to 84 degrees F. Below 70 degrees activity is minimized and over 84 degrees the fish become visibly uncomfortable—74 degrees seems to be about right. At higher temperatures, they seem to age much faster too.

Bettas, given the above environmental conditions, will provide many months of pleasure. However, you should not allow too great an emotional attachment to develop. Nor should you feel too badly if a betta is found to have passed away suddenly and before he should have. As with any other tropical fish, death or disease in bettas can occur for no obvious reason.

If you can find them for sale or have the space to raise them from eggs, brine shrimp are a truly marvelous food for bettas. They encourage activity and are a great source of several important nutrients.

However, when well kept, bettas do very well. There are very few diseases or problems that might plague bettas.

Should a problem occur, ask your dealer for a solution. Usually if a problem occurs, one or more of the environmental conditions have not been kept up. Overfeeding and its concomitant, water pollution, probably cause more disease problems in bettas than any other single factor.

LONGEVITY

Most betta enthusiasts seem to be of the opinion that bettas have an expected life span of about two and one-half years. But of course all averages reflect extremes, and information from several sources indicates that bettas can live much longer. The greatest extreme thus far tells of several males over nine years old—and still going strong! These fish live under laboratory conditions and are part of a university experiment on longevity. Each fish has a tank of several gallons to itself. Each day the fish are exercised by being chased about the tank for a prescribed period of time by a student involved in the experimen. These fish are still capable of spawning. Many of their counterparts have been autopsied and have been found to have died of fatty degeneration of tissues and organs. They had been kept in confined quarters, such as jars. Perhaps there is a lesson here for all of us, including authors!

BETTAS—A COMPLETE INTRODUCTION

Spawning Bettas

Much has been written about spawning bettas. Much of it tells of quite limited experience and deals, usually, with first experiences. The one bit of truth that might be distilled from all of these is that bettas are very easily spawned. However, the conditions given the fish in these many accounts are so widely divergent that one can only conclude that bettas have to be among the easiest egg layers to spawn for the fish to put up with the many varied conditions and still spawn successfully. It is true that bettas are, indeed, quite easily spawned, but enough can go wrong and enough surprises can come along to make it interesting and challenging.

ENVIRONMENTAL CONDITIONS FOR SPAWNING BETTAS

It was once said that bettas will, in the wild, spawn in the little bit of water that oozes up into depressions made in the soggy soil by hooves of passing water buffaloes. This is not too far from probable. A correspondent writes that in rainy weather water had flooded his basement, sometimes leaving an inch or so of water in puddles. One time he found that adult bettas had jumped from their jars and spawned in the water on the floor. To say the least, he had a time netting new fry! He also said the adults had slithered across the floor from one puddle to another, half in and half out of the water.

The writer once, quite by accident, put a pair of bettas together in a quart canning jar when water was being changed. The spawning was successful and the fry raised. Bettas, therefore, are not too fussy about the amount of water provided for the spawning. They have spawned, as was said, in a very small amount of water and also in the standard-size tanks available to hobbyists. The trick is to understand what advantages and disadvantages might accompany the use of a container of any given size.

The spawning obtained in a quart jar was successful because both fish were ready to spawn and responded to one another advantageously when they found themselves together. Had one or the other partner not been ready, there would have been no spawning and, worse yet, frustration could have been vented on the reluctant one. This can happen in any container, but the smaller the water space the less chance there is for the reluctant fish to get away from the other's amorous or angry advances. Some experimentation has shown that the water space most conducive to successful spawning of bettas in all of its many aspects is one that provides from two to ten gallons of water. These have been neither too small nor too large for the various

Male common bettas build large bubblenests even when not in the company of a female. The nests often start under a floating plant.

factors that must be considered when placing a pair of bettas together. The most usual container used is a regular aquarium, but other kinds of containers have been used successfully. There is no doubt that bettas might be spawned in opaque containers, for bettas apparently need very little light for spawning. In the Orient, enamel pans and ceramic bowls are used. The secret seems to be that the container and its water space should not be so small as to crowd the pair too much and not so large that they continually lose each other.

Water Temperature

The water in the breeding tank should be warm to increase odds of getting a spawn. Spawns have been reported as low as 64 degrees F., but the greatest percentage of successes will come at higher temperatures; that is, from 75 degrees F. to 84 degrees F. This range of temperature surely reflects temperature tolerance in the wild. Certainly, a 20-degree range is not unusual in the animal world. The condition of the breeders seems to be the most important factor. Fish in good condition will probably spawn at temperatures they are accustomed to or with some slight rise in temperature. The fish seem to be uncomfortable above 84 degrees F. and are reluctant spawn. Excessive heat will cause eggs to develop too rapidly and the fry to be weak, and in many cases, the fry die before becoming free-swimming.

Covering the Spawning Tank

Dry or cool air is detrimental to the bubblenest and to the fry, so it is best to cover the spawning tank, thereby preserving both heat and humidity. A glass or rigid plastic cover will do nicely, or you can use one of

Sponge filters work well in a betta bowl, allowing even a small volume of water to be efficiently filtered. They also are used in aquariums holding fry.

the flexible thin plastic sheeting materials usually sold for food preparation. The covering does not seem to be necessary when the room used is warm and moist. These conditions are usually found to exist in rooms used especially as fish rooms by breeders.

Aeration and Filtration

Neither filtration nor aeration is considered necessary. In fact, they can be considered detrimental to the well-being of the breeding fish and to the resulting fry. Turbulence caused by either can make nest maintenance difficult and can scatter eggs and fry. The fry seem to be very uncomfortable in moving water. They seem to thrive best in still water. Siphoning and replacement of water serve the purposes of aeration and filtration. This should be done every two or three days, particularly if uneaten food accumulates.

Light

A little light, it seems, is better than a lot. Strong

sunlight or strong artificial light can be detrimental to eggs and fry. Clear water and bright light may be convenient for observations by the fish breeder, but one should keep in mind that waters in the wild are not necessarily clear and probably not strongly lit, due mostly to floating plant leaves.

I use twenty-five watt bulbs over 5-gallon breeding tanks. Light is left on while eggs are being tended and before the fry are free swimming. When fry are swimming the male is removed and the light is turned off over these fry from then on at night. Occasionally lights have been turned off while nests were being tended. Sometimes the results were disastrous and sometimes not. If some light was present, all was well. Very little light seems to be needed by bettas.

Water Conditions

Water that is about neutral and not too hard is best, but these fish have a fair tolerance to differing water conditions. If one is aware of extremes in local water one can compensate for them by aging, adding neutralizing agents and so on. Simple aging suffices for many parts of the country.

Water Level

In this breeder's opinion the importance of a shallow water depth in the breeding tank has been highly overrated. I have used all kinds of containers, from plastic shoeboxes to 15-gallon aquariums. Many water depths have been used, and none seems to make much difference. In the plastic box, it was about 3 inches and about 12 inches in the 15-gallon tank. There are very good reasons given for starting with a shallow water depth. One is that the fry, when hatching, have a tendency to fall. If the water depth is not too great

BETTAS—A COMPLETE INTRODUCTION

they do not have very far to fall and can usually make it back up to the nest on their own. However, even a fall of twelve inches does not seem to harm fry.

Lying on the bottom of the tank does not harm them either, and they can wait until the male picks them up and puts them back into the nest. Spawns have even lain on the bottom until the yolk sacs were absorbed and then have swum normally. Breeders using a shallow water depth add water in small amounts daily after the fry are on their own until the container is full. Siphoning and replacing of water in a full container will serve somewhat the same purpose.

Snails

Snails have been reported to be a menace in a breeding tank, but such has not been the case for the author. Snails have not been observed eating eggs. Snails clean up uneaten food left by fry. Snail droppings are more easily siphoned out than is

Bettas show their best colors only in clean water. Pollutants and wastes cause dull colors, ragged fins, and lingering death.

uneaten food. Snails "seed" a breeding tank with eggs left when a tank is set up for a new spawning. Snails keep a tank in good condition longer than would be the case without them. Snails are much underrated. The common ramshorn and mystery snails have been used in my breeding tank.

INTRODUCTION OF THE BREEDERS

Placing the fish together without crowding them and without the prospect of placing one or the other in danger is accomplished in many ways and they have proven to be successful in varying degrees. Some breeders use a partition of glass or plastic in the breeding container to separate the male from the female. The fish can see but not hurt each other. The partition, of course, is removed when a nest appears and the pair of fish appear to be ready. Another popular method of separation is to place the female in a jar, which is then floated in the container holding the male. A disadvantage to this method is that if the female is ready she might drop her eggs in the jar if she is not released soon enough. The happy medium is to provide refuge for the female so she will not be harassed by the male, but her readiness will not be frustrated by barriers. She needs to be able to retreat to safety if his advances are too aggressive. Small quarters magnify the danger. A gallon jug, for instance, does not leave much chance for retreat, even though gallon jugs have been used successfully as breeding containers.

One of the most successful separators is plants. A harassed female can retreat behind plants, and even though a game of tag may take place, she can usually

Keeping a male and a female together in a large aquarium often works well, but two males can never be kept together, even in the largest tanks.

keep from being harmed. The plants provide a less restricting separator than a divider or a jar, since the female can decide when she is ready to approach the male and does not have to depend on the breeder to release her at the right time. Floating plants are the most convenient to use and are very effective. Rooted plants can serve the same purpose if planted thickly enough. Floating plants have proved to be so effective that where they have been quite thick, the female has been known to retreat after spawning only to return repeatedly to the nest site to spawn again and without harm. This has occurred three or more days after the first spawning. Fry would be hanging in the nest or beginning to swim when the pair spawned again. Research in this area has not gone much further than this, but an interesting projection might be that a pair of fish might be allowed to spawn in this manner, existing together in the same container, spawning

Putting two male bettas together leads to gill flaring and vicious attacks on the fins. One male will be dominant and may severely damage the other male.

when they are ready, and all the breeder need do is remove fry to rearing tanks as they become large enough to net. Of course, the adults as well as the fry need to be fed well. The females have not been observed eating fry, as the fry can escape the female if the plants are thick enough. She must struggle through in order to pursue them and they are fast enough and small enough to elude her. The male will eat food offered but does not seem to eat fry. He does continue to mouth the fry, but as they grow, they come to resent his attentions. When a male has been used on a continuous basis such as this, he seems to preserve the instinct not to eat fry even though he may be tending fry of various sizes.

A unique and intriguing method used by a breeder was to use a guppy trap for the female. The trap, of course, was hung inside the container and, as might be expected, the water level was high. The breeder planned to use the trap in the same way a floating jar is used. However, to the breeder's surprise, females have jumped out of the trap and joined males to spawn. On one occasion, a female actually jumped back into the trap after spawning. Bettas can jump, and the only problem this method might present is that the males could very likely jump into the trap with the female. This, by the way, has also been tried by another would-be breeder, but the problem of cramped quarters would again apply to the possible detriment of the female. Some breeders have taken a cue from the killie people and have found that spawning mops serve well as refuges for female bettas in the breeding tank.

THE NEST

Almost any aspect of the conglomerate of betta lore can become a topic of controversy. If one learns

Two female bettas may fight when confined. Today even female bettas often bear brilliant colors, though never rivaling the male in finnage.

anything from working bettas it's that nothing about them can be taken for granted. Not too long ago I would have been content with the idea that male bettas blow bubbles and that the eggs are placed among the bubbles. However, the more you learn the more you can become interested in something like the bubblenest. On occasion, someone will ask a question that should be easy to answer but seems to raise more questions when an answer is attempted. In fact, the bubblenest specifically has served as a subject of inquiry in university studies. The following comments on bubblenests are offered to give some idea of just how interesting they can be.

We humans exhibit much humor about romance, the boy-girl game and so on, but it appears that the fish aren't kidding one bit about perpetuating the species, even from youth on. Betta breeders have observed young males barely two months old, just newly in jars, frothing them up. (Did you hear the one about the lady who changed her betta's water daily because it kept foaming up?) I have not tested it, but you might wonder whether these miniature males might be capable of spawning, if they are building nests, and whether females of the same age are capable of producing eggs.

Nests in jars are indicators of good, healthy fish. Bettas in need of a change of water lose interest in nest-building. A change of water stimulates nest-building. Also, when strange males are placed next to each other, separated in their respective jars, the activity of excitement seems to stimulate nest-building. Males, rather than females, were used in university experiments for stimulation of nest-building.

During spawning, the female's eggs drop toward the bottom of the tank and are recovered by the male, who brings them to the surface to place them in the bubblenest.

A conclusion might be that nest-building prompted by sight of another male may be a strong one and may relate to the procuring of females on a competitive basis. Indeed, the characteristics of behavioral activity appear different when two males are "squaring off" in their separate jars and when one or both has a nest built in the jar. Rearrange jars occasionally to get the fish to exercise. A similar response is seen when strange females, placed next to the male, cause the excitement that promotes nest-building.

Research by university investigators has revealed some interesting bits about nest-building. Some significance is given to the idea that nest-building is at its best when the barometer is changing. Also, there is some evidence that nest-building is affected one way or another by seasonal changes. Both premises have been confirmed by the experiences of a number of breeders.

Temperature of the water is a great stimulator of nest-building, but the rigid 80 degrees has served as an oversimplification. The fish have been known to build nests from around 64 degrees to around 84 degrees. What seems to be more important is the temperature the fish are accustomed to and their general health and demeanor. Bettas given good conditions of water, food and quarters will spawn in the 70's range. A few bettas once were forgotten in the car for several hours in winter and were found later in water that had cooled down to 45 degrees. They appeared dead, but a very slow gill action was noted. When allowed to warm up gradually they revived. Several had nests built within 24 hours. Bettas in very good health will probably spawn when put together if the above conditions are met and maybe even if they are not!

Nests themselves can be extremely varied. Some males will build virtually no nest at all and still be successful. A male might just ball up the eggs in a mass with no conventional nest. Another will build a nest covering a considerable amount of water surface area and another will be content with a smaller nest of considerable thickness. Also, one male will start building a nest at the sight of a female and another only if the female allows herself to be bred.

The male will continue to build a nest even through and during a spawning. And he will continue to do so while the eggs are developing. Most of the time he will start to enlarge the nest as the eggs hatch and as the young begin to move away from the central area of the nest. Some males have been known to almost cover the surface of a 5-gallon tank with a nest. Eggs

BETTAS—A COMPLETE INTRODUCTION

Males carefully attend the eggs in the bubblenest while they develop, returning to the surface any that drop. There is more air at the surface and the temperature is higher.

sometimes are pushed well up into the bubbles of a nest so that it is difficult to determine whether a spawn really took place or whether the eggs have been eaten. Others will clump up a batch of eggs under the nest bottom.

Many breeders have found that something floating will soon have a nest built under it. An occasional male will ignore it, but most will build under such things as a floating plant like water sprite, Amazon sword plant, or even lettuce. Others use a piece of wax paper or plastic food wrapper and even bottoms of plastic cups or plastic lids of various kinds. There are other possibilities. However, university investigations of this, again, have produced some interesting results. Experimentation has shown that, to build under, males prefer something that is round, about the diameter of a grapefruit and yellow in color. These findings were checked out and were found to correspond with a floating leaf mass of types of water plants found in betta waters in Thailand. The colors red and green were less popular among males, and blue was rejected almost completely. They also found that the bubbles nourished and attracted infusoria.

Occasionally when a pair of fish had not spawned they were removed and a new pair introduced. There was some doubt expressed that a male newly introduced would use the nest left by the male removed. However, never have I observed the slightest reluctance to use nests already present in breeding tanks. The new males just added to the nests and went on from there. It's almost as though they assumed they had built them and had no second thoughts about adopting them as their own. Only rarely will a male reject a nest present in a breeding tank.

A male commonly mates with several females, so a nest may contain a mixture of eggs and fry from more than one female.

THE SPAWNING

Providing that all the previously mentioned general requirements are met regarding water, temperature, the container and so on, the breeders can be introduced. The following generalized description of the spawning of bettas is offered only as a guide. Do not be surprised if there seems to be some deviation from or variation in the pattern at any point. In fact, each male and female will exhibit some deviation, individually or as a pair, which leads one to assume that some expressions of "personalities" of the fish have to be involved, particularly when spawnings are attempted.

The spawning ritual, however, is so impressive and beautiful that to merely describe the pattern of behavior in a completely objective way would be to leave out what will be, for the breeder, an experience to be enjoyed repeatedly. Therefore, the following will move through the spawning pattern with the fish and will start with the assumption that the pair is loose together in the breeding tank.

1: The moment the fish discover each other is a moment of transformation. There are almost instant expressions of mutual awareness. Fins and gills are spread wide, and the fish's colors become increasingly brightened as you watch. It is fascinating to watch the usual horizontal barring or lack of any barring pattern of the female melt away to be replaced by a vertical barring pattern. This is a signal of her awareness of the male. They will swim side by side at this time in a trembling, pivoting kind of pattern. This will be interrupted from time to time, but will be repeated.

2: An increase in excitement then follows with the male becoming increasingly aggressive, which results in his slapping at the female with his body and fins and making headlong lunges at her in an attempt to bite and nip. Usually the female is adept at dodging these lunges and manages to keep away from real harm. It's surprising to see how fast these fish can move when they have to.

3: The female will retreat from these advances, and when the male finds he has nothing to chase he will begin to build the nest in a select spot in the tank. However, if the female swims back into view he will take up the chase once more. When she is hidden from him, again he will go back to nest-building.

4: As the nest progresses and time goes on, the male will change tactics; his approaches to the female will be more to lure her to the nest than to attack. He will swim for her, present a side view with fins and gills spread, and wag his body back and forth in an "S" pattern. He then will swim back towards the nest to lure her all the way to the nest. She may follow, but it can take some time for the male to lure her all the way to the nest. She will follow part of the way and then retreat. The male will occasionally seem to lose patience and will nip her out of annoyance. In quiet moments, he will continue to build his nest.

5: If she is inclined to spawn, the female will approach the male at the nest. She will show her readiness by swimming toward him in a head-downward position, fins clamped, and with a shimmy or snakelike swimming pattern. The vent is quite visible at this time.

6: The male recognizes the female's submissive approach. He spreads gills and fins but becomes gentler.

7: The pair will circle, nosing into each other's sides. The female is turned upside down, with the male on his side, curved over her body. The vents are in proximity in this position. Activity ceases momentarily. The very

Males are very attentive to their nests, and occasionally a female may aid in taking care of the eggs.

first embraces are usually eggless. Sometimes some experimentation is necessary for the pair to complete embraces. Once eggs begin to drop, each embrace will usually produce eggs in numbers from 1 or 2 to 50 or more.

8: The male usually recovers from the embraces first. When he releases the female she floats toward the surface on her side, seemingly paralyzed. The female recovers slowly; she then rights herself and often assists in egg gathering.

9: When either partner decides to terminate spawning the female will retreat from the nest. The male will tend to the nest. Many breeders remove the female at this point.

10: The male will mouth the eggs, push them up among the bubbles, repair and enlarge the nest. He sometimes will build another nest elsewhere in the tank and move the eggs to it.

11: The eggs hatch in 24 to 28 hours. The fry will hang tail-down in the nest for another 36 hours, when they will gradually take on a horizontal swimming position and begin to wander from the nest area. The male will tend them during all this time and will do all he can to corral the fry in the nest area. Many breeders remove the male at this point and leave the fry on their own.

As was mentioned above, there are deviations from the pattern at any point, and even though some of the deviations can be frustrating to the breeder, and even tragic at times, they can be very interesting and many times can spell the difference between success and failure. The following are some of the deviations one might experience and some suggestions for making the pattern more interesting.

The male enlarges his nest the whole time he is actively breeding, which may be several months a year. Some males build gigantic nests that cover the entire surface and are several bubbles thick. Others build tiny nests.

Deviations in Step 1.

Occasionally when a pair of fish are placed together one or the other may not respond. Sometimes a female will seem to respond to the male only to shrink away later. It is not a good policy to place either fish into the breeding tank much before the other. Either one can come to feel territorial about the tank. It is better to introduce them to the tank at about the same time. This can save wear and tear, particularly on the female. It takes a minute or two for the fish to adjust and one should not be given an advantage over the other. If a female continues to be reluctant but appears to be ready otherwise, she can sometimes be coaxed to perform by the introduction of a second female into the tank.

On occasion, it can be the male who does not respond. Ready females have been known to take out their frustrations by attacking the slow male, sometimes killing him. A very shredded and cowed male is the usual outcome. If a female retains her horizontal barring she will probably also behave in a negative way to the advances of the male. If this happens it is best to remove the fish and try others.

Deviations in Step 2.

If a male becomes overly aggressive and the female is being very badly treated, she should be removed and allowed to recuperate for a few days before trying to use her for spawning again. A good indicator of the female's distress is when she lies on the bottom of the tank gasping. She is either exhausted from all the chasing or wounded or both. However, a female is not in distress simply because her fins become split or frayed or if a few scales are missing. There is no need to worry if the female can retreat to safety whenever necessary. Some damage to fins will occur to both partners almost every time. Some battling seems to be normal. Younger spawners are, of course, more vigorous, and more damage is likely among them than among older spawners. Occasionally a spawning will occur that is beautiful in its gentleness and perfection.

Deviations in Step 5.

Spawning may begin from an hour or three or more hours or even several days from the time of introduction. Most pairs will start spawning in 24 to 48 hours. If a spawning, however, does not occur in three days, it might be wise to change partners. Sometimes changing the male will do the trick. The male might be changed if he shows only little interest in the female or does not build the nest. This might appear to be stating the obvious, but occasionally a male behaves in this way but may suddenly decide to spawn after all. It seems that the behavior of the female toward him will provide the catalyst. It may be that she had not been presenting recognizable signals to the male. In fact, the vertical barring may prove to be the most important signal. Another university experiment produced interesting results. A reluctant male was prompted to nest-building and spawning when the female he had been sharing a tank with for several days was painted with vertical bars. (From a lecture by Dr. James Braddock, Michigan State University, East Lansing, Michigan, February, 1967.) In addition, the experimenters also felt, after much statistical research, that there is a tendency in a male to prefer females of the color of the female he spawned with the first time. This might be referred to as a form of "imprinting," Now, it is not as important that the reader accept these findings as it is to be aware of them. I personally had much question about them but have not really tested them.

Some males are overly aggressive, not only flaring gill covers at a female but actively attacking her. Such males may injure a potential mate or even kill her. Whenever you place two bettas together, keep an eye on them for a while to see how they react.

Deviations in Step 7.

The experimental embraces may very well decide the fate of a spawning. Sometimes a pair will not seem to be able to perform successful embraces, and frustrations quickly end activity. With other pairs, one partner, usually the male, is able to gain position, but the other cannot. In these instances, the female is not flipped over. She then is not able to function as she should and usually no eggs will be released. Such a female soon loses interest and retreats. With others, the female will continually be repulsed by an overly excited male no matter how many times she tries to approach the nest, and she finally will retreat. Both females may release eggs in another part of the tank, and the only frustration then belongs to the would-be breeder.

When there is a great variance in size between breeders there can be difficulties too. One deals in odds when presenting a large female to a young male. Embraces are difficult if not impossible.

Experience seems to be important too. There is some indication that if bettas are allowed to age without spawning or if there are long periods between spawning opportunities they tend to be reluctant or unable to spawn. Fish that are spawned frequently seem to spawn more readily and with more ease. In fact, particular pairs tend to become quite amenable to one another, which might tempt some to label them as "mated pairs." Given opportunities, however, either partner will in all probability mate with other partners.

Deviations in Step 8.

As was said, the first embraces may be eggless. However, with more embraces eggs begin to fall.

After spawning, the female needs at least a few days of rest with good food and no male company. Males, on the other hand, may spawn with several females in succession.

There is no predictable pattern to the number of eggs dropped per embrace, but we can say that, in general, the number of eggs will generally increase with more embraces, and a dwindling of numbers of eggs will accompany completion of the spawning. One embrace may produce eggs and others not. One embrace may produce two eggs and another a veritable storm of thirty or more. The next may produce none.

When there are many eggs falling the male has all he can do to catch them all. In fact, he may have so many in his mouth at times that as he takes more in, eggs come out of his gills. Females will help gather eggs if they get the chance. The male will try to catch them before the female can. Females will scan the bottom for eggs, whereas the male sometimes will ignore eggs that have hit bottom. Eggs caught or picked up by the female are spit up toward the nest as she rises to the nest for the next embrace. Either partner may hold

Most species of betta don't build bubblenests. Instead, the male picks up the eggs and holds them in the mouth while they develop. *Betta bellica* is one of these mouthbrooders.

eggs in the mouth through the next embrace before placing them into the nest. Probably the best reason for removal of the female after spawning is that she might try to eat fry when they start swimming. A small spawning may include from 25-50 eggs and an average spawn from 150-300 eggs. Spawnings of 1,000 and more have been counted and recorded.

Deviations in Step 9.

Many breeders are content with the idea that when a pair has spawned all that can be expected has been accomplished. However, experience teaches that this is not necessarily true. Removal of the female after a spawning may assure that that particular clutch of eggs will be protected from her, but recent experiences of a number of breeders point to the idea that bettas, if fed well and regularly, could spawn literally constantly— and probably do in the wild. A male might pick a spot in a rice paddy or tank, build a nest and spawn with females as they present themselves. Eggs will hatch and fry will mature and leave the nest. Females will come and go. The fish will feed as food presents itself. Several breeders of bettas have had multiple spawnings of particular pairs at short intervals. As a result we might assume that female bettas, if fed well and regularly while in the breeding tank, can and will spawn every three days or so. In fact, one breeder has proved this to be true time and time again. Interested primarily in patterns of species continuance, she keeps adult pairs in small tanks; they spawn at will, and the tanks are alive with fry of varying sizes and ages. The tanks are choked with floating plants, such as hornwort, which makes pursuit of the fry by the adults too difficult. Males will exhibit "tending" behavior as long as they remain in this environment. In fact, occasionally a large fry will find itself caught, mouthed, and unceremoniously ejected. One could almost see the indignation the fry felt!

Betta foerschi is a large, strikingly patterned mouthbrooding betta that seldom is available to the average hobbyist. All bettas come from Southeast Asia.

The good care of the fry shown by males is often exhibited by females. Almost all females will assist in egg gathering and will spit eggs up to the nest, where the male will take them over. Females have also been known to "take over" when something has happened to the male or he has deserted the nest. A very interesting spawning took place recently that the author had never seen before. A pair spawned on Sunday. The female was not removed. On Tuesday, the male was tending a nest of newly hatched fry. The female was found to be under a nest in an opposite corner of the tank. It was first assumed that the male might have built the second nest, as some males do. But the female was observed not only blowing bubbles to enlarge the nest and repair it, but she was also catching her fry as they fell from her nest and was spitting them back up into it. On Wednesday, the female was found to be back spawning again with the

A brightly colored, very long-finned male betta cruising around the aquarium with gill covers flared and ready for action is a wonderful sight.

Because bettas breed so readily and can produce so many fry over a short period of time, this has led to many mutations becoming available to breeders. Some of these mutations include incredible body colors and fin shapes.

male. She gave up a clutch of eggs that seemed slightly smaller in number than the first time. When spawning was finished, she retired to her side of the tank. At this point, she was removed, as the fry were very important to the breeder. The male was removed two days later with some of the fry from the second spawning still hanging in the nest.

On another occasion, two females were used with one male to hopefully increase the possibility of success. It was hoped that the female most ready would spawn and the other could be removed at that point. However, after one spawn neither was removed. The first spawning had been observed. The next day the male was found to be spawning with the second female. She was a different color from the first. This has to be considered a rarity, since this has occurred only twice in ten years. Normally the protective behavior of the male would probably not let the male permit the approach of another fish to the nest that soon.

Betta imbellis is a wild betta that is very similar to the wild *Betta splendens*. Unlike the common betta (*B. splendens*), it is difficult to breed and has produced few mutations as yet.

Cambodian bettas were among the first striking color mutations to become popular. Their pale bodies and often brightly colored fins make for a great color combination.

Deviations in Step 11.

As eggs hatch fry occasionally will fall from the nest. Most recover quickly and seem to jump back up into the nest. Others continue to fall and are caught in the male's mouth and spat back up toward the nest. The male is usually kept quite busy, but a really good vigorous spawn has a very small percentage of "fallers." Some spawns will have a high percentage of "fallers," even to the point where the male gives only token attendance to the fry. Usually as the yolk sac is absorbed, the fry lying on the bottom will begin swimming about normally. Sometimes an entire spawn will result in fish that will never be able to swim normally. These fish do not seem to be able to feed and soon die off.

BETTAS—A COMPLETE INTRODUCTION

Raising the Fry

FEEDING FIRST FOODS

As soon as the fry start moving about on their own, they will be on the lookout for food. There is a great controversy among breeders of bettas as to what types of foods are best as first foods for betta fry. Basically they are split into two camps. One group believes that unless infusoria is fed to the new fry only disaster can be the result. Then there are those who have found that the new fry can and will eat newly hatched brine shrimp right from the first. The controversy will probably go on forever, but the following bits of information are offered so that you might be aware of them; then you can experiment and decide for yourself.

To state the argument in reverse, I have never used infusoria. Newly hatched brine shrimp has been the only food fed to new betta fry for more than ten years, and thousands of bettas have been raised. A number of other breeders agree with this procedure. However, to state the case thoroughly, it must be said that those who use infusoria (or other first foods) instead of newly hatched brine shrimp have had similar success. It must be admitted also that some individual fry may not be large enough to eat brine shrimp and may be lost if something smaller to eat is not present. If they are lost the breeder will never know what they might have had to offer. However, using newly hatched brine shrimp can assure almost complete success. Those who report using infusoria switch to brine shrimp just a few days later. The need for using infusoria is probably highly overrated. There are probably many infusorians present in the tank used for spawning. Researchers say that the bubblenests attract infusoria. Fry in the nest feed on the yolk sac for three days. During this time they are also learning to eat, merely snapping at random. By the time the yolk sac is gone they know how to eat, so fry are probably eating infusorians that just happen to be present. However, fry have also been observed tearing live shrimp apart.

It is very interesting to watch fry eat shrimp. The fry's transparency provides proof that they can indeed swallow whole baby shrimp. A magnifying glass is handy. The fry should be fed in amounts to assure full, rounded bellies most of the time. It is difficult to say exactly how much and how often they should be fed. But some observations by the breeder will soon create feeding habits that will accomplish full, rounded bellies and rapid growth. This optimum feeding program should, however, be accomplished without fouling the water by overfeeding. Shrimp not eaten will soon die off and decay will cause water pollution. This can quickly affect the fry, and they will quickly die off or

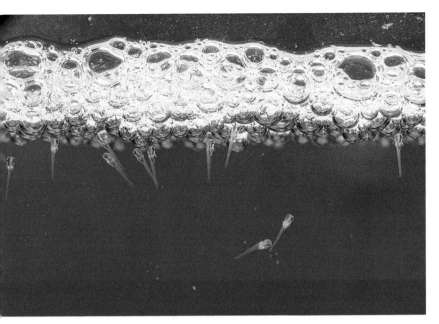

Betta fry are tiny, nearly transparent slivers that hang from the bubblenest for several days before becoming able to swim.

show signs of disease. Siphoning of the dead shrimp and replacement of the water will ensure that pollution will not occur. Use a narrow gauge siphon such as plastic air line tubing (1/8" gauge) so as not to siphon fry as well. Siphoning and replacement of half the water every few days is beneficial.

Many would-be breeders complain that a successful spawning has been lost after a week or two. On questioning, it appears that their feeding program during this time has been disastrous because of uncertainty. Most are not sure about infusoria or the various substitute tube products. The usual result is overuse and toxic water. Feeding brine shrimp is visually easier to control and is successful.

A light source close above the water will draw a concentration of infusorians or shrimp to it. Fry will congregate and feed. New fry seem to prefer food that is alive and moving. As fry progress in size and age other foods can be offered.

Methods and materials for hatching brine shrimp eggs are readily available, and the eggs are easily hatched. However, when it comes to creating and perpetuating a truly functional infusoria culture it seems we have been laboring under some misinformation. Lettuce, hay and rice media will produce good infusoria cultures if they are "inoculated" with infusoria obtained from biological supply houses or the sediment from a well-established aquarium.

Good cultures do not spring up spontaneously. They have to be made, and they have to be made well...and once they are set up and producing, they have to be maintained. Once established, going cultures can be perpetuated only if they are given the same kind of attention that worm cultures are given. Provide food for the microorganisms, keep environmental conditions good and keep numbers down by harvesting.

MOVING FRY TO LARGER QUARTERS

Fry spawned in limited quarters should be very quickly moved to larger quarters. Even if the fry are given frequent water changes and good feeding, small quarters will soon slow their growth. Small numbers of fry have been raised to sexable size in small quarters, say ten to twenty in a gallon of water, but when 200 to 300 fry occupy five gallons of water they will soon stop growing if not moved to larger quarters. A rule of thumb is to provide a gallon of water for ten to fifteen fish. Weekly water changes and generous feedings will produce rapid growth. The fry should be moved to large enough quarters so they will mature enough to sex at two months of age.

When fry are ready to move from the breeding container to larger quarters it is all right to siphon off most of the water and pour them gently into the larger container prepared for them ahead of time. I move fry from 5-gallon aquariums to 15- or 23-gallon aquariums. A betta farmer in Florida moves spawns from gallon jugs to cement pools 6' x 6' x 2'. The pouring does not seem to harm the fry. In fact, pouring gently is better for the fry than netting. Filtration at this point is desirable, but it should be gentle. The fry are still sensitive to moving water. I use inside corner box filters.

At a recent meeting of the local betta club, a new member observed that she has two tanks of betta fry being raised. In one of these tanks she has placed a number of guppy fry. She has observed that the betta fry in the tank with the guppies have been much more active and lively than the betta fry in the other tank. In the other tank the behavior was much more sedentary, as is more typical of bettas. Another observation was that the betta fry in with the guppies were getting larger than the betta fry in the other tank, even though they are all the same age. I have no explanation, nor does the breeder, but it is an interesting phenomenon and may have significance.

Covering of the tank is also desirable if the room is not heated. When the fry are about five weeks old, their labyrinth development will bring them to the surface for air. There is much evidence that chilling (a good degree of difference in water and air temperatures) is detrimental to betta fry and a major cause for wholesale losses of fry. This has often been reported, but I have never experienced it, perhaps because of the warm and humid conditions in my fish room.

Two different conditions have been a problem for me after the time when the fry are transferred to larger quarters. One, it is assumed, seems always to parallel the time when the fry start using the labyrinth. At about this time some individuals in some spawns will be seen swimming with difficulty, with tails dragging. This condition has been reported by breeders all over the country; these fish have been referred to as "fallers" or "jumpers." Some have destroyed these fish, but almost all of them, in almost all cases, overcome it as time goes on, and they gradually come to swim normally. They feed and grow and appear only to be uncomfortable. The problem is with the swim bladder. These fish appear to have a shorter or less developed swim bladder than those that continue to swim normally. Those that have suffered the condition and overcome it can be observed to finally have developed the swim bladder to the necessary length and size. From then on they can be considered normal fish. There is no real evidence that the condition is hereditary. No one has yet found a truly satisfactory cause or cure for it. One writer suggests putting affected fry in a container with very shallow water. This would eliminate the need for the fish to struggle so. The rest might facilitate overcoming it. On rare occasions, an adult fish will suddenly show symptoms, and it might be assumed that it is a recurrence of the condition. Almost none of those fish will overcome it

BETTAS—A COMPLETE INTRODUCTION

again, and they are best destroyed. For them swimming is too difficult and life is too uncomfortable. The best advice seems to be, if the condition presents itself, that the breeder saves only those fish that do not seem to suffer from it or those that get over it quickly. It depends on the importance of the particular spawn.

The other condition is "velvet," a parasite. Fry from a few days old to sexable age of two months are most susceptible to it. Symptoms of "velvet's" presence are inactivity, clamped fins and congregation at the surface or on the bottom; on close examination, tiny yellow spots will be seen over the body and on the fins. It is usually most obvious on the pectoral fins, which are usually clear or transparent. By this time, the disease has been with the fish for a few days. It is difficult to spot in the early stages because changes in behavior are slight as the parasite takes hold. Bettas given good conditions should not contract "velvet." Some breakdown in environmental conditions weakens the

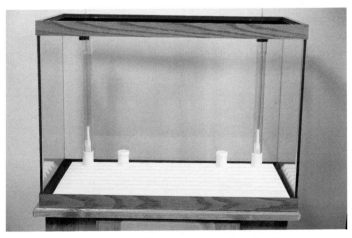

To raise a decent spawning of bettas, you need to give them an aquarium with a low water level and adequate but not too strong filtration. Cover the tank to assure the surface air stays warm.

Many betta diseases are most obvious in the finnage. Though tears may result from just normal activity, diseased bettas often display very irregular fin edges that appear to have been eaten away.

fish, and the disease takes hold. Fin-clamping is the most obvious sign, since appetite is not affected at first. The organism producing the condition seems to be present in the water, but it is not recommended that the water be medicated as a general rule. Treatment of the disease when seen on the fish or when symptoms show themselves is recommended over treatment of the water just because it may be present. Healthy fish do not need to be medicated.

The treatment of betta diseases is usually quite simple if they have not progressed to a point where no treatment is going to help. Clean water conditions, of course, provide the best preventive, but on occasion, a problem may appear even under the strictest care.

TREATMENTS FOR COMMON BETTA DISEASES

The treatments I have listed here are those that have worked (with varying degrees of success) for me.

Other hobbyists prefer to use the commercially formulated medicinal preparations available in pet shops, as they're a lot easier to use in most cases.

Velvet

A complete change of water coupled with the addition of one tablespoon of non-iodized salt for each gallon of new water can reduce this menace to a mere annoyance. In a day or two, a marked improvement should be noted. If not, repeat the procedure. Of course, the filter should always be changed.

The quantity of salt in the water will not be detrimental to the fish, but it does appear to kill the parasite. A change of water alone is not always sufficient. Some writers advocate excluding light, since the parasite relies partly on chlorophyll production. To depend on this as a treatment, however, would not be wise.

Fungus, Tail and Fin Rot, Lip Infections

Net the affected fish and apply mercurochrome to the affected areas only. Do not apply to gill areas

Fry and young bettas seem to be especially subject to velvet, ich, and similar diseases caused by protozoans. They simply are delicate at these ages and often also are overcrowded.

directly. Put the fish in isolation in a jar of clean water. Look for signs of improvement and repeat treatment in three or four days if it seems necessary. Lip infections seem to require repeated treatments—perhaps three or four. New growth of fins may come in clear or of a different color than they were.

Ich

Use the same treatment as for velvet.

Fin Ailments

Fry in their first three weeks are susceptible to a fin disease. The tail and pectoral fins will turn white and appear to stiffen. The cause is usually pollution of the water, and a water change will usually clear things up in a day or two. If this is not done, the fry will die. Small white patches on the bottom of the container show where dead fry have decayed.

I am often asked why the fins in adult bettas become ragged. This seems to be quite puzzling to the fancier, and in most cases, some questions must be asked in order to attempt to find a cause. Was it something that happened overnight or over a period of days? Is it a splitting between the rays or a diminishing of length or size from the outer edge? Were plants present and, if so, what kinds? Had any conditions been introduced that were new or unusual within the betta's container? It always helps to be able to see the fish in question.

Bettas often will become ragged from the unusually vigorous activity accompanying the spawning ritual. This is natural and should not cause concern. These tears will close. The fins of the betta are only a few cells thick, so tears in the fins from activity can be likened to the fraying of the edges of a flag flapping in the wind. The same kind of tears from activity may

The longer and heavier the finnage of a betta, the more likely that it will have at least a few splits in the thin membranes between the rays. Such splits are not indications of diseases.

occur if a male in his jar is placed near another betta or sees his reflection in a mirror. However, this sort of tearing is unusual and is not inevitable. Tears or splits between fin rays can also be the result of parasitic attack, such as velvet. This is more to be seen in very young bettas.

Fin rot is another major cause of deteriorated fins. Combat this condition with commercial medications available in pet shops or by swabbing the affected parts with mercurochrome. Repeat if needed in three or four days. Fin growth will be rapid and as good as new in a week. Do not be surprised if new growth is lacking in color.

On occasion, a betta will seem to lose pieces, strips or sections of fins, seemingly overnight. No one seems to know why this happens. However, this is a rare condition. Fins in this condition should not be expected to regenerate well.

Both sexes of bettas start life looking much alike, but males soon develop longer fins and more belligerent personalities. Young males must be given separate containers to prevent injury.

SEPARATION AND ISOLATION

At about two months of age, some individual fish will be easily identified as males. Sparring and nipping in very short encounters will take place. These are usually not serious or damaging, but it should be kept in mind that if males with undamaged finnage are desired they should be isolated at this time. This has been accomplished in various ways.

The most common method is to isolate males and sometimes females one to a container. Glass containers are the most commonly used. Quart, half-gallon and gallon jugs are used. Different breeders prefer certain sizes. It is not long before many jars will be occupied by members of a spawning. The problem with jars is that each must be treated as a small aquarium and must provide the fish with the environmental conditions to its best advantage: clean water conditions and food in good quality and quantity. Quantities of jars containing fish eventually must be changed. No breeder using jars has yet reported a methodology that makes water changes unnecessary. Various procedures have been developed by breeders for water changes relative to individual circumstances.

The writer has a counter area about eight feet long with a drain centrally located. A funnel tops the drain and is fastened to a length of garden hose running from the funnel to a drain in the floor. The fish room is situated in the basement. Clean jars are grouped to one side of the funnel and jars needing changing on the other. Fish are netted as dirty water is poured down the drain and the fish placed in jars of clean water. These jars are then placed back on their shelves.

The fish continue to grow in their jars with weekly water changes and good feedings, and it is possible to raise them to an excellent mature size in these jars. The writer has used only quarts and half-gallon jars and has found that it cannot be claimed that small jars will diminish the size potential of the fish—if other factors, as outlined, are meticulously kept up. Many other species of fish would be badly affected by such cramped quarters, including other anabantoids, but not bettas. Perhaps this can be better understood and accepted if we keep in mind that for a long time bettas have had to get along in the various water conditions found in the wild coupled with the fact that they are labyrinth fish. There is the story told that thousands of bettas are raised in the Orient in tin cans. Cans are punctured many times and strung or wired together in a group. They are wired to a raft which keeps can tops above the surface, and the many holes allow water circulation. Live food, especially mosquito larvae, presents itself by swimming through the holes. This is truly fish farming. It produces a harvestable crop.

Some domestic variations on this theme use plastic bags in place of tin cans. The trick is to provide large enough containers in which the bags can be suspended; refrigerator liners, plywood troughs, boxes, or cement pools have served the purpose. One breeder suspends many plastic bags on metal rods. These are then suspended in the water in refrigerator liners. Males occupy the bags while females swim free in the liners. The bags are well perforated, as are the tin cans. Another breeder uses plastic bags suspended from plastic floatation collars. The bags float free in large cement pools. Females again swim free.

With modern plastics and plastic resins, plywood tanks have been built and thousands of bettas have been raised in them. Boxes of any dimensions can be built and lined with plastic film or fiberglass or painted with plastic resins to waterproof them. One breeder built plywood boxes 4 feet wide, 8 feet long, and 8 inches deep. They were built in tiers of three, like bunk beds, one above the other. They were lined with painters' plastic drop cloths and served well.

Small plywood or plastic boxes have been built and fitted with plastic dividers to provide space for a number of male bettas. These were designed as pilot models for replacing jars and their demands. The large boxes (4 x 8 feet) were envisioned fitted with many compartments, but this was never done. It remains for others to find the ultimate emancipation from jars whether it be plywood, plastic or tin cans. It is still in the future for domestic breeders to give Oriental breeders a bit of competition at least to the degree of producing crops of bettas with the seeming ease that conditions provide there.

A while back, a reward was offered for the apprehension of a rehabilitated betta—one that had given up the ways of violence and could be trusted to get along well with others of its kind. Maybe someday someone will latch on to this elusive character, but until this happens we might just like to consider some of the interesting aspects of this question.

Anyone who has raised a spawning of bettas knows that between the ages of five to eight weeks certain individuals in the tank population will begin to show aggressive tendencies toward others in the tank. These encounters do not seem to be sex discriminating at this point—they just pick on whoever is closest. Skirmishes are brief, usually, and the damage to either fish is usually slight. Sometimes three and even four fish will constitute a battle. The stimulation of activity is too much for some, and they just have to join in. Because these skirmishes are brief and without too much damage you must wonder about the mechanics of them.

One breeder has always had mature males and females coexisting in large tanks of about 50 gallons in size. Spawnings of bettas are raised together in these large tanks. Males are removed only as fish are sold or as jar space becomes available. These fish are forced to coexist. Encounters are constant, but their short duration and lack of serious consequence are significant. The only obvious disadvantage to be seen is ragged fin edges on some males. Other males show little or no damage; females seem to be fine, as they seem to be subject to attack less, will avoid a challenge more or assume a submissive (or less territorial) attitude in a situation like this. The fish are "harvested" from these tanks as needed, as was said, and nipped fin edges heal fairly well in a short time after they are jarred.

This breeder has not kept records of how long bettas could be kept together in this way, but there is no reason to doubt that these fish could go on living together throughout life, given the opportunity. Bettas in his tanks in some cases have been at least six months old. He gives his bettas the best of conditions—clean water and plenty of good food. He uses heavy filtration of the tanks and changes the water completely at least once a month. He also provides floating plants in the tanks, and he occasionally has bubblenests dotting the surface in the tanks. He has seen fry in these tanks, evidencing that spawnings have taken place in a community situation. Might we say that in his tanks we are seeing a microcosm of what might be seen in the wild? I am inclined to think so.

My conclusion to this is that bettas might be raised together if they are raised together from a very small size. This condition must continue unchanged for best results. After the first three weeks or so no strange fish should be introduced into the group. The introduction of any strange fish at any time after this can be disastrous to at least some individuals, including the strangers. Once initial skirmishes are over, however, (perhaps one day) strangers are assimilated into the group. These skirmishes may be territorially oriented, but calling it a pecking order might be a better way to put it. This would be interesting to research more

Sometimes very stable tanks that are heavily planted will allow you to keep a few young males together, but any disturbance could lead to a disaster.

conclusively. Also, fish that have been removed from the group will be treated as strangers on reintroduction into the group, even after only one or two days. Males removed from the group and placed in separate jars will fight each other through the glass, as they never did while among the group. Even females will do this. So, removal from the familiar experiential-spatial situation to one new and unfamiliar, as well as disruption of the familiar situation, in some way will trigger a very much increased intensity of the fighting stimulus. Quite often pet shops will bring in female bettas and will find that when the females find themselves together in this new situation they will begin to spar with one another. This may be why female bettas are considered difficult to keep alive in pet shop tanks. They can wound one another, infections such as fungus can take hold, and dead fish can be the result.

Another stimulus to fight is new or different water. This may be another reason why females will fight each other when placed together in tanks in pet shops. The water is new to them and probably is well filtered; it may even be new water, as when tanks are newly set up to receive new shipments of fish. The stimulus to fight is quickened when males are placed into clean water. This is always observable on changing them from old or dirty water to new, clean water. As water becomes older, activity is lessened, only to be stimulated again with a water change. This can also be observed in a tank of females when all or part of the water they've been living in is changed. Short skirmishes will break out all over the tank; this will continue for several hours and then taper off.

Hobbyists have on occasion raised spawnings of bettas in outdoor pools in summer. They have reported co-existence, probably because of the greater surface

Many hobbyists think that male bettas show their best colors when allowed to spar with another male.

Older bettas (30 months or older) often begin to look senile, with sagging, split fins and irregularities around the head. Bettas, under normal circumstances, are not especially long-lived.

area than is found in the usual aquarium. No out and out fights were reported. The usual encounters consisted of approach, threat, and retreat.

A researcher interested in the fighting behavior of bettas once took two males to the middle of a lake and dumped them overboard. Instead of swimming away from each other in this relatively vast expanse of water, these two fish fought! Apparently, the amount of water space is not as important as to decide who is "king of the hill" in this new situation. This is probably the reason why bettas fight when introduced to one another. The setting is probably new to both fish and some kind of outcome must be decided. Most often, those who stage betta fights are disappointed in the performance of the supposed antagonists. Bettas commonly available are not necessarily imbued with all the fighting prowess one might hope for. Bettas are selectively bred in the Orient for this one characteristic, and losers are not used again for breeding.

BETTAS—A COMPLETE INTRODUCTION

Buying Bettas

Betta splendens has undergone a great transformation since it was first kept as an aquatic pet. The resemblance to the wild form and coloring is slight; the finnage has been bred to lengths resembling flowing drapery rather than fins. Colors have been sorted out until we have fish of single solid colors, and the colors have been intensified. Over the past few years, coloring and color patterns have come into being that could only have been imagined before. In addition, bettas are known to be one of the easiest egg layers to breed, and they offer a breeder great potential for color breeding.

Most pet shops carrying tropical fish offer bettas for sale. When looking over the offerings, be discriminating; shop around. However, don't discount your esthetic reaction to particular fish. Trust your reactions to general proportions, purity of color, mixture or distribution of color, beauty and condition of fins and demeanor. The following suggestions are made to help you, the betta purchaser, get the most for your money. They are made primarily with the male in mind but refer, in general, to the female as well.

Many times I have shared a hobbyist's joy over the purchase of a betta, only to realize on seeing it that the fish was far from the ideal specimen the hobbyist's enthusiasm made it. Some general knowledge of form and proportion will give the hobbyist the kind of discrimination he might want to use when purchasing a purebred dog or cat...he should be aware of what others consider ideal.

AGE OF THE FISH

When purchasing bettas, try to find out the ages of the fish purchased. Young specimens between five and eight months of age are in their prime for breeding, and this makes them desirable. Many of us succumb, sadly, to showy, fully-grown specimens and risk having them to enjoy for only a short time. The younger fish will be with us longer. It is very enjoyable to watch the fish grow and change as time goes on, and with proper care, a betta can give much pleasure for several years. Also, the younger ones are better potential breeders, generally, and would be available longer for breeding purposes. Younger fish usually are also of greater vigor, and they show it. They tend to be more active and aggressive. Individuals just over three months of age have proved that bettas can and do produce good spawns at that age. Older fish become less active as time goes on and do not tend to be active for periods of time comparable to those of their younger counterparts. Look for activity if the age of the fish is in question. The presence of a nest can be an indicator

No all hobbyists like bettas with extremely long fins. Few casual keepers would challenge the statement that these blue bettas are truly
beautiful fish.

of youth but is not a surefire sign, nor should it be
taken as an absolute indicator of ability or inclination
to spawn. If the fish appears willing to fight his
neighbor, he may be a good candidate for purchase.

The most successful way, of course, to obtain fish of
a particular age is to get them from someone (either
their breeder or someone who bothered to ask their
breeder) who knows how old the fish are. Often
superior stock can be obtained in this way. Often a
good fish from "unknown sources" can be had from
pet shops. Most of these fish come from the Orient via
Florida, California and New York. Fish farms in the
Orient produce hundreds of thousands of bettas
yearly, and although most of them are quite commonly
colored and formed, the perceiving eye can on
occasion find an exceptional fish for breeding
purposes.

Occasionally, young "unsexed" bettas will be offered for sale. Look for the most obviously healthy, active and aggressive youngsters. Color should be a secondary consideration unless one is taken by a particular color. Do not sacrifice vigor for color. If the unsexed fish seem to be of good proportion, finnage and demeanor, as well as color, they will, if given good conditions, give much pleasure as they grow—and they will be ready for spawning in a very short time. Knowing age will be helpful. Some breeders feel that bettas are most ready for breeding at six months of age. However, as was said earlier, bettas just three months old have been bred successfully. Some breeders report that bettas two months old can be bred successfully. The extreme is the report of bettas just six weeks old having been spawned. This I have not tried, but a conclusion might be that we wait too long to start breeding. In fact, there is some evidence that if bettas are kept from spawning for long periods of time they show more reluctance (or inability) to spawn. Conversely, bettas that have been spawned periodically prove to be more successful spawners.

FINNAGE

A fullness of fins as well as length to the fins is most desirable. Long but narrow fins, for instance, can indicate poor stock or poor rearing conditions. There is a desirable length of fins to look for, but fullness indicates a better fish. Look for a roundness of the caudal and an anal fin that extends from just behind the ventral fins and seems to meld with the caudal. Look for abrupt changes in direction in the fin rays; they might indicate that the fins at one time were damaged or diseased. Look for a very light or very dark edge to the fins, as this very often will indicate that the fins still have some growing to do. Fin rays that extend just beyond the growing edge of the fins seem to indicate good robust stock. A folding or draping effect in the fins, sometimes even when spread out, indicates good stock. A ragged appearance to the fins is undesirable. We might also take a cue from the guppy breeders and reject those fish, which appear unable to carry their finnage.

Most hobbyists are aware of the existence and popularity of Libby bettas. Warren and Libby Young of New Jersey proved that size in bettas could be enhanced through selective breeding. They stressed the importance of care in choosing the most advantageous females for breeding. Males, of course, are easier to select. The popularity of their bettas has resulted in the name "Libby" having become synonymous with largeness in bettas.

Wild bettas, including the ancestors of the common betta, *Betta splendens*, had short fins without striking beauty. This is a male *Betta imbellis*, very similar to wild *Betta splendens*.

Care in the selection of fish for breeding cannot be stressed enough, and it must be understood that a would-be breeder must not expect instant success. A true breeder is one whose persistence and desire to learn in order to overcome obstacles are very strong. As a matter of fact, some who read this might not wish to just simply pursue the usual goals. They may want to challenge the popular concepts of quality and create new ones.

The most usually seen caudal form is the so-called "veiltail," or melon-shaped caudal, although today other caudal fin shapes, such as the roundtail, are becoming increasingly popular. Other forms for the caudal might include a "pintail" or pointed form and also a "delta" form. Both are being pursued by breeders. The "delta" form seems to be an elusive one and some more definite research will need to be done with this form. It seems to have a spread toward the edges of the caudal and is more or less squared off at the outer edge.

It has been suggested that a breeder might increase his chances to improve his stock by meticulous counts of fin rays in dorsal, caudal and anal fins. Variances do occur and may be transmissible. Speaking of rays, some see advantages to recognizing extensions of fin rays, and examples of this have been referred to as "combtail" or "fringetail" bettas.

The aberrations of form above may produce our future excellent bettas. Some deficiencies in form have been forwarded as desirable, but the opinion I hold is one of skepticism. To attempt to perpetuate such as a lack of the dorsal or the ventral fins, I think, is less than desirable. Such might not be the case if an

Male or female? Sometimes it is hard to sex colorful female bettas or males that have small finnage. Many breeders go more by behavior than by color and shape.

exaggeration or doubling of fins is encountered. Double-tail bettas, for instance, not only sport double tails but also have dorsal fins that are double in horizontal width, having almost double the normal number of rays. These have proved to be transmissible qualities. It seems that many of the qualities seen in fancy guppies and goldfish can help us to foresee form qualities in future bettas...and to their advantage.

PROPORTION

Proportion of the body to the fins is very important. A large-bodied fish with relatively short fins will most likely not develop long fins. In fact, these males can sometimes be mistaken for females because of their short fins, and they have caused hobbyists some real consternation when set up to spawn with other males! Occasionally these males will be true throwbacks to the wild form but possess the more sophisticated coloring.

A very slim-bodied fish with seemingly good fins may be exhibiting the results of disease, poor inheritance or dietary and other environmental deficiencies. It is difficult to say just what ideal proportions might be, but an extremely slim body is to be avoided.

BASIC CELL COLORS AND COLOR VARIATIONS IN BETTAS

Color is pretty much a matter of taste, so not too much can be said about what you should select—but a few suggestions can be made as to how you might select for color. Most of the bettas on the market possess more than one color distributed quite randomly. They are usually very nice fish and make worthy additions to community tanks. However, if you are interested in breeding for solid color, for instance, it is worth the time and effort to seek out individuals that are decidedly one color in body and fins, or closely so, for to start with breeders of mixed coloring you are set back immeasurably.

Certain new varieties of bettas becoming available include those with dark bodies and lighter colored fins. Examples are blacks or browns with yellow fins. They have become known as bi-colored bettas. Another bi-colored betta, the Cambodian betta, has been with us for many years; it has a light pink body that can be combined with red, blue or green fins, and its versatility can be carried on further to include Cambodians with black, yellow or white fins.

Such versatility of color is possible not only in a given group of bettas but even in a particular spawning when spawning for a particular color pattern. One of the great joys of working with this fish is to be surprised with the outcome of a particular color spawning for the subtle variety to be found in the fry. Conversely, this can be quite disconcerting if your sights are set too narrowly for the outcome. It is better simply to enjoy the range of differences and, of course, those individuals that do approximate the imagined goal. Yellow, red, black and blue bettas exist because selective breeding has produced them. Yellow, red, black and blue have been found to be the basic cell colors in bettas. Selective breeding has altered and intensified the distribution of the desired color cells while diminishing or inhibiting the others, thus creating "pure" color strains. Nondiscriminating breeding of bettas produces the randomly colored mixes we see so often.

Yellow cells (xanthophores) lie deepest. Red cells (erythrophores) overlay the yellow. Black cells (melanophores) are found overlaying the red, and crystalline cells (guanophores)—which produce the green and blue we see—are found closest to the surface. The Cambodian lacks color cells in the body. The fins of this color mutation are usually fully colored, but even this manifestation has begun to give way to those breeders who would manipulate the fish's color or color pattern.

Cambodians exhibit very sparse populations of yellow, red, black or blue cells over a background color found to be a combination of color of tissue, organs and blood. Thus, the cleanest of Cambodians would possess a quite even salmony or pink-beige coloring coupled with colored fins. Any intensification of any of the above-mentioned color cells will produce a Cambodian body that appears pink, reddish, pale blue, pale green, yellow, etc., coupled with fin colors mentioned. However, understanding of betta genetics is yet rather primitive, and to project such combinations as pale green with yellow fins, for instance, will probably have to wait before it can be done with any degree of certainty. But an understanding of what we do know will bring an increase in and control over manifestations of color such as mint green, suggestive of the luna moth. A betta was once seen that was of that coloring, but it was not spawned.

It is a fascinating experience to observe color cells in bettas under the microscope. The most useful seems to be a dissecting microscope. It allows for low magnification, which seems to transform the fish's coloring, while maintaining the image of the fish. Those bettas possessing iridocytes appear to be sprinkled with glittering bits of color.

Under the microscope, color cells might be likened in appearance to freckles in humans. Their sizes, colors, intensities, depths and numbers vary. Looking at a portion of a betta's body under the microscope reveals varying concentrations of particular color cells known as "populations." Heavy populations of one color produce the naked eye vision of singularity or intensification of that color. Under the microscope a red Cambodian, for instance, would reveal a spotty distribution of red cells that may look quite even by naked eye observation.

Under the microscope, fin coloring may reveal differing concentrations of color cells on the rays and on the tissue between rays. This difference may or may not be apparent via naked eye observation. If you ever have the opportunity to look at bettas under the microscope, don't pass it up; the experience will be with you the rest of your days.

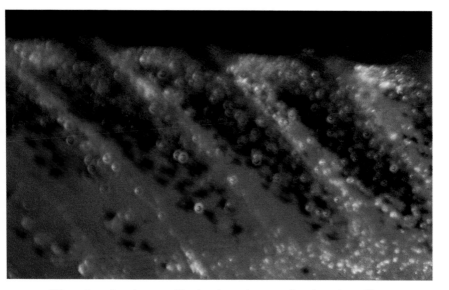

When viewed under magnification, it can be seen that the colors of bettas are not uniformly distributed but instead are localized in pigment clusters that overlie each other to produce a spectrum of shades.

Many bettas appear to be green, and this might be considered to be a basic color in bettas, but greens seem to exhibit an elusive color. Many people do not see green but shadings between turquoise and blue. The deciding factor, however, seems to be that the green is highly iridescent, a shininess or sparkle accompanying the color. This is not true of truly blue bettas, even though blue is produced by the same cells that give us green. If green bettas are compared side by side with blue bettas, the difference is easily seen. The gleam of the green classes the green as green, as distinguished from blue.

The following descriptions are given to suggest how variable color in present *Betta splendens* individuals can be. They represent color varieties that do exist. It is not suggested that the listing can be taken as complete, for new ones are coming along all the time. The key is that those listed can be spawned for with a good degree of predictability. Fish exhibiting or carrying the color or color pattern must be used, of course.

On rare occasions you will find a betta that appears to have extremely strong coloring that is all pervading, quite even and with much depth. This is true in reds, greens and blues. In fact, these individuals often seem to be so "full of color" that even the pectorals are fully colored. (In most cases, the pectorals are clear and not showy.) In these highly colored individuals, the constant motion of these fins is observable. This is a characteristic well worth working for.

Red

Solid red or "candy apple" red coloring has a clarity and depth that make it one of the most brilliant reds one might expect to find in bettas. Bettas so colored often have colored pectorals.

This may be a red betta, but it is not very attractive because the colors are dull and uneven. Sometimes these problems can be overcome by improving diet and keeping conditions.

Varying amounts of black pigment cells produce blood reds, tomato reds and maroons. These reds can be quite velvety looking. Darker reds often have concentrations of black cells edging the scales. A further intensification of black cells over red can be produced by selective breeding, and the result can be a very dark-bodied fish with red fins. Such fish have been produced and named "firefins."

A red-violet can also be spawned for, given the proper breeders. It is a red with a very evenly distributed coating of blue cells over the red.

A true orange does not appear to exist thus far, but tendencies to yellow-orange can be seen in the yellows. Some day we may have orange bettas.

Blue

There are basically two blues, dark blue and steel blue.

Dark blue (sometimes referred to as "cornflower" blue or "royal" blue) is a deep, basic blue that can tend toward a blue-purple. This is a tricky color to work with. When blue is mated to blue, only a portion of the fry will be blue like the parents. The rest will be divided between steel blue or green. This is due to a partial dominance in blues. A researcher tells us that a spawning of steel blue and green will produce all dark blues.

Steel blue is basically a deep blue with an over-all silvery sheen. The fins are quite silvery too. It has also been known as "gun metal." A mating of steel blue to steel blue will produce steel blue.

Green

Geneticists tell us that the iridescent green color is produced by waste products. They also tell us that the "iridocytes" (the cells that produce the color) are crystalline in form. A general term for these cells is "guanophores." They tell us too that blue is transmitted to our eyes by the same kind of cells, but something about the cells' structures determines whether we perceive green or blue. This is true not only in our beloved bettas but also in birds, like the blue jay.

However, the green in bettas is a beautiful green-turquoise coloring, with much depth, that is iridescent, reflective and shiny. A mating of a green betta to a green betta will produce green bettas.

Cambodia

A Cambodian betta is basically a salmon or pale pinkbodied fish that displays fin coloring in the above colors. Slow to take on popularity with hobbyists, this color variety catches the fancy of the breeder because of the possibility of breeding into it the fin colors of one's choosing. The fins can be made to possess a single color, two colors or even three colors. One that I had for a time, before it decided to become disorderly, was referred to as "bunting." The fins were vertically banded in red, white and blue, reminding one of the bunting hung at political conventions. Any Cambodian coloring can, in general, be perpetuated by a spawning of like Cambodians. Cambodian is recessive to the colors mentioned above.

Black

The black betta has been with us only a relatively short time, so you might have difficulty finding it. However, if one is found do not be surprised to find that the black of the black betta is not the black of the black molly. Depth and intensity of the color seem to come and go

Though sometimes considered a yellow, the brownish body color of this betta reduces the impact of the yellow fins. It probably would best be called a brown/yellow. Few casual keepers would call this a beautiful betta.

as the mood of the fish changes, more so in this color than in any other. The color is at its best at the time of spawning. Then the color is reminiscent of a shining blue-black chunk of coal. At other times the color fades and wanes like the stripes of an angelfish. There can also be varying degrees of iridescence over the body. You might prefer to eliminate the iridescence to obtain the blackest black possible, but it is quite attractive.

Yellow

Yellow bettas can vary in the yellow range from a very pale yellow to an orange-yellow. This can be very even throughout, or the fins can be a paler yellow than the body. The color can also be enhanced by blue or green fin bases. Varying degrees of iridescence can be present on yellow bettas; this pattern is very attractive. However, in a competitive show of bettas, the most buttery yellow betta over-all would win the trophy.

Black/Yellow

When I first saw this combination, it was difficult to accept. A light body with darker fins, yes—but not the reverse. There seems to be much variance here too, from a pale brown body to an almost black body. The fins can be pale beige to a buttery yellow. The yellow can also approach orange. The fins can be fully colored or translucent. They can be black-edged, which is very attractive, or possess the blue or green fin bases mentioned in the yellows. In fact, suspicion proved out. A mating of black/yellows provided a percentage of all-yellows. A spawning of black/yellow to yellow gave an approximate 50-50 split between the colors.

You might surmise that these are yellow fish with an increased (to varying degrees) population of black cells, more or less limited to the body. The population of yellow cells underneath the black also varies, creating the great variability in the body coloring. This variability is increased again when these fish are seen possessing high numbers of iridocytes, producing blues and greens with yellow fins. These fish, as do the all-yellows, do not seem to be able to produce red pigment. It seems to be missing. Dr. Gene Lucas of Drake University in Des Moines, Iowa has dubbed these fish and all-yellows as "non-reds." A highly iridescent green body coupled with yellow fins is a striking fish indeed. The "non-red" phenomenon has exerted a great influence on the evolution of color in bettas in the last few years. The non-red gene as a "known" has made it possible to develop greens and blues that, visually, are greener or bluer because of the lack of red cells. Even Cambodian types have been affected. The basic yellow betta has exerted a genetic influence. The non-red effect is to remove the betta one step further from the wild coloration, which exhibits much red. Non-red bettas, especially the blues and greens, are bluer and greener because red is not present to affect the quality of the color in the fins, in particular, and the ventral fins especially. A Scottish visitor to my fish room several years ago asked me the question, "Which fish is more desirable? One with red in the ventral fins or one without it?" At the time, the question confused me, and I answered badly. I said, "With red." Bad answer. If a blue fish or a green fish is most desired, then one showing little or no red is most desirable.

Black, yellow and black/yellow bettas are still rare. Reds, blues, greens and Cambodians are easier to find. Those showing mixed coloring are even easier to find. However, if only these were to be listed, the betta's versatility would not be truly recorded. The following colors also exist, but only in a limited way, some in an

This true yellow betta has not only bright yellow fins but a similarly colored body. The color is uniform and bright, making it a nice fish for the specialist.

experimental sense only, and they are not generally found on the market.

Brown

The brown betta is a reddish-brown fish with black scale edges and translucent black fins. It is not really a spectacular-looking fish, but the very fact that it exists and can be perpetuated is interesting enough.

Cambodian-Black

Several years ago, I attempted to combine the Cambodian body coloring with black finnage. As interesting as it was, it became one of the most frustrating crosses I ever tried. A Cambodian female was mated to a black male. The result was a batch of fry exhibiting all of the usual colors, but none were black or Cambodian. This was, of course, expected in the first generation, as both black and Cambodian give way to the commoner colors expected to be lurking in the genetic background of each fish.

A second generation from a brother-sister cross produced an approximation of the imagined goal (cream-licorice). The frustration arose from the persistent paleness and irregularity of the black in the fins. This refused to improve with passing generations. Only the beauty of some of the individuals made working on the strain worth the continued effort.

Today some breeders report possessing individuals that exhibit the combination with improvements. The intensity of contrast has been improved, and enhancement has been made more sophisticated. There have even been reports of Cambodian black/white butterfly types. I have often indulged in speculation as to how many variations in color and pattern might be possible in bettas at a particular

The pale straw body and light but brightly bicolored and very long fins of this elegant betta are typical of what commonly is called a butterfly betta, a type of Cambodian.

moment, but the creation of a list usually proved to be short-lived as a definitive list. But I found this exhilarating—certainly not frustrating!

The black, brown and Cambodian-black strains all suffer a malady not known among other colorings in bettas. Females phenotypically black, brown or Cambodian-black seem to be incapable of providing viable eggs. (Phenotypical means that the fish exhibits the color or color pattern being discussed; they show their color). A fish that appears black is phenotypically black. It is a black phenotype. A red fish is a red phenotype. However, a fish that is exhibiting a color but is known to be of a particular color strain different from the color exhibited is known as a genotype. An example: often a breeder's strain of blacks will include females that are phenotypically red, blue or green but genotypically black. They are used to carry on the strain. In the black, brown and Cambodian-black it is

Notice the double tail on this Cambodian betta. Doubled tails in bettas often also lead to greatly enlarged dorsal fins with twice the normal number of rays. Both features are linked in the genes.

not known whether the eggs are incapable of being fertilized or whether something happens in the early stages of egg development. Large clutches of eggs are laid, but they always fungus. This problem has been dubbed the "lethal factor" in blacks and related strains. Breeders have reported this malady from many areas across the country. Females phenotypically of colors other than black, brown or Cambodian-black but genotypically black (that is, they can transmit the color to offspring even though they don't show it themselves) were used to carry on the strains. Approximately 25% of the fry were of the desired coloring working them in this way. This is why there aren't many, if any, of these strains on the market; few people will rise to the challenge of a small success ratio.

Clear Fins

Some individuals in the brown, yellow and the

variegated strains have shown a tendency toward a lack of any color in the fins, which leaves them quite clear, almost like cellophane. Spawning for this lack of color has brought some success. The variegated strain also exhibits a tendency toward white fins as well as clear. Clear-finned bettas have been offered commercially as "cellophane bettas," which is quite apt.

Gold

The development of the gold strains was an outgrowth of the Cambodian-black cross. A few of the first generation were iridescent green, and a sparkle of gold was noted in the pectorals of some. A second generation (brother-sister) revealed both green and Cambodian fry that grew to possess a golden shininess over their bodies and into the fins. The fins were primarily red, however. Pectoral fins in some were solid gold. Subsequent generations have reduced the red

Compared to the normal round tail of most bettas, double-tailed bettas often appear ragged, with uneven tail fins and rough edges to the other fins.

A truly gorgeous double-tailed betta with bright, iridescent colors and long, even, flowing fins that are carried well on a large body.

and enhanced the gold. An interesting sidelight is that the fry, when about two weeks to one-month-old, look very much like little brass nails.

Variegated (Butterfly)

The title "butterfly" is borrowed to describe a color pattern that appears to be quite spectacular in bettas. It is presently applied to Cambodian, red, green and blue-bodied strains that possess fins with colors divided more or less evenly between color and white or clear. The fin coloring can vary greatly from almost colorless to an abrupt "painted" division of color, to an extension of color into the fin rays, giving the colored area a saw tooth or serrated look. These patterns are very unstable in that perhaps only 25% of a spawning may show it. The rest are commonly colored.

Several breeders gave the butterfly title almost simultaneously to bettas of the above descriptions. The decisive criterion seems to be a color-and-white division in the fins. Body colors could be any color combined with fins partially colored and partially white or clear. Those I am aware of now are: red-red/white, green-red/white, Cambodia-red/white and blue-blue/white. Many other combinations could still be created, such as Cambodia-blue/white, Cambodia-green/white, green-green/white and so on. These remain for breeders to imagine and to attempt to create. Other fin color combinations could also be projected.

Many hobbyists are often not aware of or appreciative of the history that has contributed to their enjoyment of the hobby. Nor do authors often give credits where they are due and should be recorded. In *Beautiful Bettas*, by W.L. Whitern, credit is given to Mr. Tutweiler of Florida for a truly spectacular butterfly betta. It was Cambodian with fins divided between white and red, but in this case the white was closest to

The uneven growth of the rays of the anal and caudal fins of this betta are distractions from its bright colors. The tears may be due to just normal breeding activity, however.

the body, so it was a Cambodian-white-red. This is a reverse of the pattern of butterfly bettas seen today. Unfortunately, no record is given of this fish ever having passed on his characteristics. We can assume that we have lost this aberration, as nothing exists today to equal it.

The father of the butterfly betta as we know it today is Jay C. Niel of Ovid, Michigan. Years ago "Doc," as he is known, and his wife maintained a tropical fish shop in Arlington, Virginia, and there they raised the first Cambodian-red-white butterflies. Doc is retired now and is no longer a fish breeder. My memory of him is that of the typical "Kentucky Colonel" with the typical white mustache and goatee coupled with his very amiable manner—a "pioneer" to be well remembered and revered in this hobby of ours.

Other Colors, Patterns and Fin Forms

The basic color patterns listed thus far number over

Few casual hobbyists would consider this dark-bodied, short-finned betta to be especially attractive. Some specialist breeders, however, strive for such uniformly dark colors and will later breed for increased finnage.

A very pale double-tailed Cambodian. Though such fish may be sought-after by breeders, they seldom are popular in pet shops, where casual breeders prefer brilliant colors.

twenty, but even so, they do not present a complete listing. A complete listing may never be possible. Even as this is being written, experimental spawnings are being made and new color combinations coming into being. Blacks with blue fins and green fins are being worked to set the strains, as are blues and greens with yellow fins.

This all leads one to wonder about other color combinations, and from these wonderings come the future beautiful bettas. For instance, greens with red fins have been seen but not fixed, leading one to wonder whether the opposite could be accomplished or whether reds with yellow fins or blue fins could be created. Word came recently from a breeder about yellows with red fins that showed up in a spawn.

Occasionally truly thrilling surprises come along. An albino has yet to present itself to this breeder, even though thousands of bettas have been raised.

However, in 1967 Mr. Carl Immeke of Miami, Florida found among the thousands he was raising a betta that possessed ruby red eye coloring. It appeared blind, as were the two or three albinos recorded in the past forty years. The body coloring, however, was of the iridescent yellow coloring he referred to as "platinum." At best this fish might be classified as partial albino. The most widely accepted definition of albino seems to be that it would be of a "clearish" or whitish body coloring coupled with the red eye coloring. This condition appears to be very elusive in bettas, as doubt has been cast on whether any of the reported albinos would truly fit the description. The question seems to have to do with the degree of pigmentation or lack of it to be allowed a candidate for albinism. A betta reported in 1927 was so lacking in pigmentation as to be transparent enough to reveal internal organs.

White bettas are attractive if they have a solid, dense, iridescent coloration rather than just being pale and translucent. They still are very uncommon, however, and seldom seen in pet shops.

The bright blue body and fin colors of this betta contrast with the duller brownish black head. Would such a betta sell well in pet shops? Probably not, as brighter, more uniform colors are more popular.

Its eyes were bloodshot. It was very weak and died without spawning. None of the albinos reported succeeded in perpetuating themselves. And such is the story of the 1967 albino. But now we seem to have a new albino. It was shown in the 1969 betta show in Detroit, Michigan by Mr. Rod Grimes of Dayton, Ohio. It appeared to fit the description and was accepted as such by those attending the show. It also seemed to be sighted, making it different from other "albinos."

As a result of trying to perpetuate the black-blue and black-green strains a new challenge arose: a male having a dark red body with fins divided between red and blue-black—a truly beautiful fire and smoke betta. But even though he has been spawned with sisters and aunts, none of his young have had his coloring. One of a kind? Yes. And as elusive as the albino? Perhaps. So be watchful.

Regardless of coloration, male bettas are equally aggressive. The exception occurs in males with very long fins that impede their movements and force them to become more sedentary.

Besides color versatility, however, the betta has experienced a change in form as well. Bettas with two tails are now available on a limited basis. The caudals are truly two and are arranged one above the other. Thus far, the tails do not equal the fullness or beauty of the single-tailed fish, but the potential of these fish some day will be exploited by an adventurous breeder somewhere, and the double-tails will rival the single-tails and be as attractive and sought-after as the multilobed caudals of fancy goldfish.

The double-tailed bettas, however, possess one other attribute that offers much: the dorsal fin. It is about twice as wide as that of the usual betta, starting much closer to the head. It possesses twice the number of rays as the common dorsal. The dorsal is as wide as the anal fin and almost as long. First impressions suggest that the fish might be swimming upside down. It would be a credit to the species if

Betta splendens would be readily available in many color combinations with the very large dorsal fins and double tails, very wide and very long, flowing one over the other as the fish swims. Indeed, "teasers" have been seen, and "teasers," quite often, are the beginnings of things to come. Beautifully colored and formed double-tailed bettas in yellow, bronze, black, red, blue and green have been seen. The tragedy, very often, is that these individual fish are not worked, and this very often means that the particular color and/or form aberration is lost for the period of time it might take until it shows itself again. In terms of human activity, this can often mean a great deal of time, and time is something a "turned on" breeder feels he doesn't have. Even though patience, as a virtue, is often learned, it is never accepted.

Breeding genetics of double-tails seems to reveal a classic kind of simple recessiveness, as it is usually

All betta color and finnage varieties originate as small mutations that are taken advantage of by breeders, who selectively breed to improve the variation over many generations.

understood for color. Double-tailedness is recessive to single-tailedness. All fry (the F1 generation) resulting from a mating between a single-tailed and a double-tailed fish are single-tailed. In the event that one of these mixed fry is later spawned to a double-tailed fish we would find that resulting fry (F2) would be 75% single-tailed and 25% double-tailed. Of course, the numbers reflect approximations. There are variations. However, if double-tail is mated to double-tail all fry will be double-tailed.

Much variation in form still expresses itself within the double-tail conformation. This too makes it a challenge for the breeder interested in a mutation for what it has to offer in itself. Variation in form and size in all fins and in body quality is the rule rather than the exception.

Evolution of a species is a process requiring great periods of time, usually, for effecting changes—and yet we can enjoy some dramatic changes in tropical

A dull brown female betta. Breeders do not neglect the value of good females in their breeding programs, going for females with good body size and proportions as well as interesting color shades.

Traditional pet shop bettas tend to be large, often old, males with very long but regular finnage and bright colors on the fins and at least part of the body. Many pet shop fish are multicolored, considered a defect by most specialists.

fish simply by recognizing signs and breeding for them. This is truly remarkable. We can, as breeders, work for those qualities of fin, form and color we feel are advantageous to the animal and to us in the satisfaction we derive from what we accomplish. To cite examples is unnecessary. What is important is that our knowledge of variations of color and form in bettas, in particular, will help us to breed for the changes we want and bring them about faster.

There are some late developments that bear discussion. However, to see these types it would be necessary to search out the breeders who have created them. Very few are seen in shows yet, and then they are shown only by their creators.

A group of new and unique bettas are those tagged "non-red" bettas. These can be blue, green, Cambodian and even black. Yellow bettas are generally incapable of producing red pigment cells (as well as not being able to produce the iridescent blue and green or even black). The yellow-only betta can be considered a mutation, as was the Cambodian. The yellow-only phenomenon became known as possessing a non-red gene. The use of this fish in matings has contributed to the creation of non-red greens and blues. These greens appear greener and the blues bluer. The blue and green seem to become truer or cleaner and more intense. Even ventral fins lack red, exhibiting yellow where red used to be.

Cambodians and blacks can also be produced that are "non-red." Again, the quality of color is improved. Often a black betta will be plagued with red pigment cells under the black, which makes him look "rusty" and makes him a poor show specimen. Eliminating the red and creating a "non-red" black betta will give such a fish a much better chance at a show. Black bettas often have translucent fins, reminiscent of black lace angelfish. They even exhibit spotting similar to that of the angelfish in fin bases. Breeders have responded to the beauty of this aberration and have established it as a strain, calling it the black lace betta.

Pastels are bettas exhibiting very limited and delicate coloring in the Cambodian range. Their paleness suggested the name. Cell populations are scattered and sparse so as to create the image. The title is a number of years old, and the sad fact is that breeders who coined the title were ridiculed for their vision by those who should have understood. But eventually truth overcomes!

The "opaque" betta is a phenomenon that exhibits an unusual density of color cells. However, it is not a dark type; it is a light type. The "opaque" title refers

Unusual patterns such as this black and white probably will never be accepted by average betta keepers, who prefer bright colors. When odd patterns are combined with low finnage, you have a fish that will not sell in the pet shop.

to the density of color not only in the body but in the fins as well. "Opaque" bettas are basically Cambodian types.

Last, but surely not least, is one of the newest and perhaps most unusual of the latest developments in bettas: the piebald or marble bettas. As was said earlier, credit must be given where credit is due, and, of course, the story is always interesting. Credit for the creation of marble bettas goes to Orville Gulley, an inmate of Indiana State Prison. You've heard of the Bird Man of Alcatraz? Well, Orville has to be the Betta Man of ISP. However, the creation of marble bettas was unintentional. Orville was trying to "invent" a black butterfly betta and didn't realize what he had done. At the time, he was selling his surplus fish to me and once sent a number of these fish to me. At first glance, on unpacking them, they appeared to be a very drab bunch of fish. But they had been shipped in cool

A betta to please both the casual keeper and the specialist: a brilliant red male with very uniform and bright color as well as long, very even finnage. What more could one ask?

Sometimes long fins can be a disadvantage to a male betta. In combat the males attack each other's fins, often inflicting deep tears and biting off chunks. Flowing fins are more easily damaged than lower fins.

BUYING BETTAS

Many casual keepers would call this fish a Cambodian, as it has a pink-ish straw body and blue fins. Typical Cambodians, however, have the bases of the fins pale. Today almost every possible combination of body and fin color is easily available.

weather and their water had cooled some, so I wasn't greatly concerned. (It appears that when bettas, and other tropicals, are cooled down the pigment cells contract and color is diminished). After the fish had been transferred to containers of fresh water (fresh water is often safe and exhilarating to bettas) of a slightly higher temperature they brightened up and were transformed! Then I couldn't believe what I was looking at. They were all young fish, perhaps five months old, males and females, divided between single-tails (ST) and double-tails (DT). To make the story shorter than I'd really like to write it, many of the fish were marbleized, meaning they wore their coloring in patches somewhat reminiscent of marble angelfish—hence the title. Dark patches were black, blue, green and even red. Areas devoid of color were like Cambodian. Even fin areas were affected. It seemed that a mutation governing distribution of color had taken place. Mr. Gulley did not choose to pursue the marble betta. This is regrettable. It is only speculation at this point as to what he might have done with the aberration. However, several people obtained some of his stock, and the strain is carried on today.

The story doesn't end here, though. One of the breeders who obtained stock concentrated on the marble exclusively. She found that when marbles were mated the fry were every color of the rainbow. They were red, green, blue, black, yellow, Cambodian and butterfly. The fish started out reddish and as they grew they changed to the colors mentioned. Hard to believe? Wait! Just when the fish looked like they would be great show specimens in the colors they displayed they started to change, and the changes

Though interesting to specialists, these Cambodian-like bettas are pale (pastel) with only moderately high fins. A specialist breeder, however, could take these fish and over several generations isolate the best features of the color pattern.

were observable daily. A blue fish became Cambodian, losing its blue coloring, and then picked up color to become the patchy-looking marble. A red fish became black and then lost color to become marble. It was never determined whether the fish ever stopped changing colors. It may be a while before we hear more of the marble betta, but it's only a matter of time. This fish will have its day.

It might be mentioned here that a number of prisons across the country permit and encourage the keeping of aquarium fishes in the cells of inmates who become hobbyists. Of course, prison cells permit an extremely limited hobby. A visit to the Indiana State Prison demonstrated just how limited this can be. Because of limited space, inmates become very ingenious when it comes to accomplishing what they set out to do in the hobby. A personal visit to Indiana State Prison

A deep, almost mahogany red betta. Notice that the coloration is relatively dull, however, not as iridescent as most hobbyists would prefer.

The many shades of blue and violet on this long-finned betta male make it interesting, but the spots of red scattered over the fish would be considered a defect by most breeders.

emphasized the fact that prison inmates can become as enamored of and involved in the hobby as most hobbyists "on the outside," even though they have much less space to do it in! One cell's complement of tanks, stands and whatever was so jammed in that some of the occupant's areas of natural need were rather impaired—but obviously the hobby came first! In the case of bettas, males and females were raised in small peanut butter jars. Lids were kept in place and holes through which the fish were fed were put in the lids. To further conserve space the jars were stacked in pyramidal form. This still allowed for feeding. Of course, the water was kept quite clean too.

BETTAS—A COMPLETE INTRODUCTION

Raising Bettas for Fun and Profit

Sorry about that, but I couldn't resist that old clinker as a title for this section. But as unimaginative as the title really is, almost every hobbyist who manages to breed a pair of bettas and raise a bunch of fry has toyed with thoughts of selling his surplus fish and does, at that time at least, try to combine fun with profit. Even this book is evidence of the truth of the cliché, for I never would have been able to learn and write what you have been reading if I had not been able to sell the bettas I raised.

Now there's certainly nothing wrong with wanting to sell surplus fish. Selling may even be better than trying to give them away like so many kittens or puppies. However, anyone finding himself—or herself—in the situation of looking for customers for surplus bettas should know that there are rules to be followed, particularly if the breeder expects a merchant to buy the fish. First of all, if you have perhaps fewer than 25 surplus bettas it would be unwise to let go of them if

A piece of plastic foam can form the basis of the bubblenest and is easier to maintain than living plants. If you are breeding commercially, you will have to take many such shortcuts.

you plan to continue breeding and raising bettas to sell. It would be more to your advantage to create a "stable" of breeders to work with. Also, surplus fish are best sold when they are between four and six months old. If they get too much older, you will have invested more in the fish than you can expect to get for them. However, some merchants will make a price differential between young and older, fully grown bettas. The fully-grown bettas are often referred to as "show" bettas. Also, sometimes a dealer will buy bettas younger than four months old at a reduced price. Bettas under two months old are sold as "unsexed," since they are generally too young to sex.

It is decidedly pleasant when you can sell your surplus fish to a dealer. However, remember that the relationship you create with him, in this first encounter, is most important to you. Assuming you are offered a fair price for your fish, you might be paid in one of three ways: cash, merchandise, or even credit. Naturally, it is easier and best to deal with a dealer you know, and an exchange of your bettas for an amount in merchandise is the usual result of such an encounter. And what hobbyist can say he can't use another tank or heater, food or even another betta?

Well, there's a big difference between selling your first surplus bettas and being a serious breeder-for-profit. For one thing, you have to be a consistent producer of good fish. Fish dealers are businessmen and have to think business. They are always interested in quality merchandise, and there has to be a consistency to that quality. Often would-be breeders will do well the first time around, but for one reason or another will not produce quality after that—they lack consistency, and if you lack consistency you'll lack sales, because dealers can't afford to deal with undependable sources.

To sell commercially, you will have to start off with breeding stock that is not only productive but also represents colors and shapes that will sell well in local pet shops.

Space, space, space! To breed bettas commercially even on a small scale requires lots of rearing tanks and jars for young males. Breeders have used almost every conceivable container to fill their needs.

A real sign of success is if a dealer who has bought bettas from you starts carrying just your bettas. This may happen by a kind of mutual agreement, but sometimes it will just happen. When a dealer starts to call you and says how many he needs, you have a new problem. You then have to decide whether you want to become a steady supplier. Any dealer worth his salt can sell quite a few bettas each week, if they are quality fish, with the average shop selling a dozen or so a week. If you are not willing to produce the necessary stock on a regular basis, talk it over with the dealer and perhaps you can continue an occasional supply as had been done before. However, if you agree to provide a steady supply, do all you can to maintain that supply. Nothing is more annoying to a merchant than to expect a constant supply and then not be able to get it.

If you create a good stable of breeder fish and create a good workable fish room, you can manage to supply your dealer with good quality bettas and enjoy the benefits of doing so. The costs of the creation of such an operation can be well supplemented by the sale of fish. I cannot say exactly what will be best for you, but three or four breeding tanks and as many raising tanks should suffice for a beginning operation. Shelves and jars for 200 to 250 fish will come in very handy; variables in your situation may alter these figures, of course.

Now, let's say you want to branch out and supply another dealer or two or three. Take samples in when you approach each one and be very, very sure you are going to be able to supply their needs every time they need bettas. (You should, by the way, be prepared to sell the samples; this often happens.) Don't overextend yourself and hope you will have the needed fish.

In their own way these are beautiful bettas that might appeal to a specialist, but they would never sell in the general pet shop. Therefore, they are unlikely to be bred commercially.

Prepare for this ahead of time. Have the fish on hand. Expand your operation before committing yourself. You can't build a clientele on "if you'll buy them, I'll raise some for you." That won't work. Supply is needed today, not three months from now. As each new client is obtained, expansion of supply must have been accomplished. The number of breeding tanks and raising tanks will have to have been increased proportionally. Conventional glass tanks can be used and strong metal or wooden racks need to be built to carry them. Remember that water is very heavy (8 lbs. to the gallon). Wooden racks of 2 x 4 construction are very serviceable if built well. A visit "behind the scenes" at your favorite shop will teach you much.

All-glass tanks are a slight convenience, but volume raising doesn't require their use. On fish farms, opaque-sided containers of all kinds are used for betta fry. They range from ceramic containers to cement ponds.

As I expanded my betta "factory" and it became "Bettas Unlimited" I found I needed to become very inventive so as to accommodate the amount of stock I needed to carry. The space I had available dictated that quart canning jars give way to plastic containers of a lesser capacity. I used plastic drinking glasses used in restaurants. Shelving was altered to accommodate as many as possible. The object of this operation, of course, changed from a raising activity to one of short term holding before sale. I continued to breed and raise bettas that were of special interest to me, but the bulk of those held for sale were purchased from breeders in the US, Canada, Malaysia, Thailand, Singapore and Hong Kong. There were times when I had as many as 5,000 male and female bettas in containers—and this figure was exclusive of the fish in tanks. By the way, imported females did much better one to a container than in a group situation in a tank.

Beautiful colors but low fins—-would this type of betta sell well in your town? Probably not, in which case you don't want to waste valuable space keeping the line going.

It should be mentioned here that anyone reading this who might anticipate importing bettas from the Orient in quantity must check the current importing restrictions; also, you'll have to live near a port of entry or understand how an agent can be used at a port of entry in the event you don't. In any case, insist that female bettas be bagged singly, as are the males. Females shipped together in one bag can be disaster!

Finally, as the numbers of fish in individual containers increase, help will be needed for changing water. As betta raising in the Orient is a family occupation, all family members help with this chore. My good friend Tay Hong, of Bangkok, who used to send me very beautiful bettas, had two wives. When he visited here, he was asked which wife was "No.1." He said it was the wife who was "up-country," because she helped with the fish! My older children all took turns earning their spending money changing water.

Piebald or marble bettas often have interesting patterns and, oddly, continually change their patterns and colors as they grow. Could they sell well locally? Perhaps a few would be worth the space to find out.

Don't forget the wild bettas and their relatives when trying to breed to sell commercially. *Anabas testudineus* often produces large spawns, and it is uncommon enough to attract considerable interest.

Regardless of whether you decide to raise a few or a lot of bettas for fun and profit, be sure to keep in mind that the greatest compliment you will receive is the reputation you can obtain if your fish are good fish. Your fish should give others the kind of pleasure you want to get from bettas yourself; that's where the real profit is!

One more item to be considered no matter what the goal of your betta raising might become: heat. A heating unit that heats the entire fish room is essential. What's best in your situation is for you to determine, but an electric heater is usually too expensive. Check with your furnace company as to your needs, and be sure you are in agreement with all building and construction codes when you install any new and additional heating units. My betta "factory" used one half of my basement, and a small gas heater served my

Though it is not especially colorful, *Betta edithae* is one of several wild bettas that attract many specialist keepers and fetch a good price. Such wild bettas, if you can breed them in decent numbers, may sell well over the internet.

needs quite well. It heated a small breeding room and a larger raising area. (The heater also had the effect of making the rest of the house warmer, and here in Michigan that wasn't bad. Shortly after its installation, our oil company came out to check why our oil consumption had dropped so dramatically.) Individual heaters will still need to be used in breeding tanks and possibly in raising tanks near the floor. Be aware that even fish farms in Florida have heating units operating in in-building areas, used especially at night. Know your particular needs and provide them.

Now, of course, quantity raising of bettas for sale is a commendable and satisfying goal as described above. While I operated Bettas Unlimited I received literally thousands of letters all saying they were not able to get "good" bettas in their localities. Unfortunately, this is often true. I think I empathized with all those hobbyists about their esthetic image of what "good" bettas should be. These hobbyists had graduated from the multicolored mongrel bettas so often seen and were looking for something better. And betta fanciers continue to search for the "better bettas." So another goal, as commendable as raising bettas for profit, is to raise the better bettas. But to do this one must be on the lookout for really good bettas and try very hard to find out where they are and who has them. There are several hundred aquarium clubs in the US and also a goodly number of local betta clubs. The International Betta Congress unites betta fanciers on a worldwide scale and can quickly bring a novice betta "nut" up to date on what is going on in bettas. If

Some wild bettas, such as *Betta macrostoma*, are spectacular but have proved almost impossible to breed in numbers. If you can get good stock and have the room to experiment, you could produce some very salable specimens of such uncommon species.

your particular interest in the species, in its present stage of development, is limited to the "special" bettas, your contribution to the "specialty bank" can go one of two ways, or maybe even both ways.

Firstly, competitive betta shows are held all over the country every year, just as are dog, cat and horse shows and, of course, other species of tropical fishes. The competition is keen and the fun even greater. Breeders throughout the country concentrate on particular specialties—colors or forms—and enter their specialties in the appropriate show classes in hopes of nabbing those class trophies. This competition tends to encourage improvement in specimens entered in the many classes in shows. A lady in Columbus, Ohio raised the very best green bettas I ever saw and won

Old-style bettas with bright colors limited to small areas and low finnage seldom sell well today when spectacular long-finned males are available cheaply in almost any store. These fish may have had *Betta imbellis* in their ancestry.

Remember that bettas with exceptionally long fins may not breed well, so the most successful commercial bettas are really a practical compromise between the very best fish and the more mundane.

many, many trophies while she was working them. A gentleman in California raised the very best yellow bettas I ever saw. A lady in Ann Arbor, Michigan raised spectacular black bettas. Another fellow, also of Michigan, had excellent luck with both yellow and black. Perhaps you would like to concentrate your efforts on green, red or blue or an opaque, marble or double-tail.

Secondly, your tastes and desires might run to the development of experimental strains of bettas, such as opaque. These types, however, usually are not salable in shops, and very often there are no classes for them in shows. It's a matter of challenge, and challenge can be its own reward. And, of course, that's where betta raising is at!

RESOURCES

Advanced Bettas
A message board devoted to betta keepers. Has many commercial links if your are looking for new fish.
http://groups.msn.com/AdvancedBettas

AquaBid
Buy and sell unique betta strains and other fishes
www.aquabid.com

Betta Webring
An interesting and informative commercial site.
www.bettasrus.com

California Betta Society
An active IBC chapter on the Pacific Coast
http://cbs.bettas.org

Canadian Bettas
If you're in Canada, the IBC chapter for you is Betta Breeders Canada
http://groups.yahoo.com/group/BBCanada

Delphi Betta Forum
Post your questions and get help from knowledgeable breeders.
http://forums.delphiforums.com/bettabreeders

International Betta Congress
The IBC is the dominant betta organization today, with many active chapters. Publishes an informative newsletter. A club for beginners and advanced betta keepers alike.
http://ibc.bettas.com
e-mail: bettacongress@yahoo.com

New York Area Bettas
Try the Big Apple Betta Breeders, an IBC chapter
www.babb.info

Tropical Fish Hobbyist
The oldest tropical fish magazine in the US today, it often publishes informative articles on bettas.
Tropical Fish Hobbyist
P. O. Box 427
Neptune, NJ 07754-9989
www.tfh.com

Wild Betta Species
There are no comprehensive sites on these, but try the following for bits of information.
www.wildbettas.com
http://home.c2i.net/philippi/Betta/betta.htm

INDEX

INDEX

PHOTOGRAPHERS

Allen, Bob
Francais, Isabelle
Frank, Stanislav
Gilroy, Michael
Hansen, Hilmar
Knaack, Karl
Lekaree, Somphongs
Linke, Horst

Lucas, Gene
Pengilley, Barry
Richter, H-J.
Roth, Andre
Tanaka, T.
Taylor, Edward
Walls, Maleta
Zukal, Ruda